RISK

FINANCIAL MARKETS & YOU

Your Guide To Making Better Investment Decisions

ALAN A. FUSTEY

ISBN: 1463525893

ISBN-13: 9781463525897

For Mary, Andrew and Meghan

ABOUT THE AUTHOR

Alan A. Fustey is a 25 year veteran of the Canadian financial service industry with experience in discretionary portfolio management, derivative securities and structuring investment strategies for high-net-worth private clients.

He is a Past President of the Winnipeg Society of Financial Analysts and his professional designations include: Chartered Financial Analyst (CFA), Certified Investment Manager (CIM) and Fellow of the Canadian Securities Institute (FCSI).

CONTENTS

PREFACE

BUY LOW, SELL HIGH, WHY IS THAT SO HARD TO DO?

"Buy low, sell high" is likely the most widely quoted financial market truth of all time. It makes so much sense, yet it is one of the most difficult tasks to repeat successfully in financial markets.

You now have access to an almost endless amount of financial information through books and internet sites. You can view television channels that are dedicated solely to providing live market information and a platform for free advice from financial industry personalities. You can contact legions of financial advisors who are more than willing to provide you with investment recommendations for your portfolio.

Has all this information and advice translated into financial success for you?

Even though most individual investors have at least a basic comprehension of what they should do for their own financial well-being, the reality is that they:

- Make their own investment decisions that produce disappointing results;

- Relinquish the responsibility for making their investment decisions to the financial advice industry without a realistic understanding of the consequences.

You don't make a conscious choice to fail to achieve your investment goals, yet that may be the likely outcome.

My belief is that most individual investors are unsuccessful because, as human beings, we are all fallible. We have engrained biases that make us prone to producing unconscious mental errors. We struggle to understand probability and overestimate the likelihood of favourable investment results. The financial advice industry uses our weaknesses against us in how they present information, make recommendations and charge for their services. The result is that we perceive financial markets as being more predictable than they actually are and, ultimately, we suffer as investors.

This book is a synthesis of the knowledge I have gained through my personal experience guiding individual investors in financial markets and through two decades of my own research.

The purpose of this book is to:

- Provide you with a better understanding of how you make investment decisions.

- Identify the judgment errors and biases to which we are all susceptible.

- Provide you with an understanding of the key premises that underlie financial market theories.

- Illustrate the cost, conflicts and camouflage that are used by the financial advice industry to further its own interests.

- Offer you investment solutions that will allow you to increase the likelihood of achieving your investment goals.

My 25 years of experience in the investment industry has taught me invaluable lessons about not only how markets function, but also about how people function in markets.

In 1985 I started my investment career as a retail broker, after simultaneously completing a bachelor degree and many of the courses that were required to obtain a licence to advise in securities. I joined a prominent brokerage firm, which at that time, were still independent and not owned by the large Canadian banks. In my local office there were nearly two dozen brokers. I was twenty-two years old and the youngest broker in the group by close to twenty years. The industry had recently removed the rule that required fixed rate trading commissions for equities, so competition from discount brokers was just beginning. Mutual funds were only sold to clients by way of an up-front sales charge that was a negotiated amount between 5%-9% of the initial amount of the investment. The devious method of hiding commission payments in the form of deferred sales charges had still not been introduced and fee-based discretionary managed accounts for individual investors were an investment option available to only the ultra-wealthy.

I completed my rookie broker training and began to strategize about building a clientele. I had limited personal investment experience, other than what I had learned from my training courses so, like my colleagues, I relied on what my employer's research department told me should be added to my client's portfolios.

My role was to provide investment advice to clients. My clients paid for the advice through the commissions that were produced from the securities transactions that occurred as my advice was implemented.

Every morning I started my day by listening to conference calls from the firm's research analysts, who touted the companies that they covered in their specific industry sector. The outlook for companies was almost universally positive. "Buy" recommendations were the norm. A company's financial prospects had to be so poor that it was close to being delisted from the exchange, before a "sell" rating was issued.

Changes in the relative outlook for individual stocks were always a focal point, as target prices were raised after each earnings release. New switch recommendations were made among sectors and stocks were *discovered* every day. Buy and hold? Forget that. It was buy; hold for a while; and then sell and try again. Although the message came from *research* analysts, the overriding theme was generating commission revenue by providing new ideas to tempt clients to trade.

During the last part of some calls, a corporate finance representative would appear, wanting to discuss a new stock issue that was from the same industry sector that the research analyst had just spoken about so glowingly. His job was to explain to me why my clients should strongly consider the *unique investment merits* of the security that his corporate client was offering for sale. The retail client base of a brokerage firm was a key cog in the firm's securities distribution network. If a sector of the equity market was performing particularly well, the corporate finance department would always produce a multitude of new security issues that would capitalize on any retail demand for investments in that sector.

I was not naïve when I joined the brokerage industry. I understood my role and that my success was ultimately a function of sales. What I didn't appreciate was the extent to which continued progress in sales volume was required to *keep your seat.* I had monthly reviews with my branch manager, but the focus was on my monthly sales production and what could be expected for his budget for next month.

Our firm tracked the monthly commissions produced by each broker on a report called the *Ladder of Success.* The ladder listed the name of each broker in a hierarchical ranking based on the monthly and year-to-date sales commissions that they had produced.

This report was distributed nationally to all the firm's brokers as a motivational aid. As I tracked my fellow brokers on the report, I could see that names that were consistently near the bottom eventually disappeared to pursue other career opportunities. Names of brokers who were near the top also occasionally disappeared, but instead they left to join rival firms. This type of career move resulted in the receipt of a lucrative payment for moving their clients and the commission dollars they produced to the new firm.

The top commission producing brokers, who stayed loyal to their firms, also received various luxury trips for achieving certain levels of annual commission production. One broker from my office enjoyed a firm sponsored vacation while he was suspended from trading by regulators for violating securities law. When the suspension and the trip ended, he resumed *advising* his clients.

I decided to be more altruistic in my approach to investment advice, so I created a retirement planning course that I taught through the continuing education programs of several local school divisions. Many of the participants in this course eventually became my clients. In addition to my retirement planning clients, I also advised individuals who wanted to trade options and commodities, which at that time were very much a niche investment product for individual investors.

As my experience in the industry grew, I learned more about the attributes of various types of investments. I completed more courses and became increasingly more fascinated with the workings of financial markets. The most valuable lessons I learned were about how individual investors mentally deal with their investment decisions and the volatility of financial markets. They liked their gains but, more importantly, they hated their losses. They viewed their accounts myopically. When their account had five stocks with gains and one with a loss, even though the total gains would more than offset the loss, the losing stock became their preoccupation. They would make excuses so they didn't have to deal with the reality of a loss: *"It's only a loss on paper; it doesn't count unless I sell it."*

It was the early 1980s and the greatest equity bull market in history had just begun after almost a decade of poor stock returns. Interest rates were declining from double digit peaks and bond prices began a steady multi-year advance. It was difficult not to choose an investment that would eventually produce a profit. Financial advisors and investors all believed that they had a Midas touch, as opposed to simply being in the right place at the right time. No one ever believed that their profits occurred solely from random luck. I was no different.

Reality hit for the investment industry and individual investors on Monday, October 19th, 1987, when an unprecedented single day decline occurred in financial markets. Neither I, nor my clients, nor other long-time advisors in my office had ever before seen anything like Black Monday. Clients, who were previously comfortable with the perceived risk that they had accepted in their investment accounts, suddenly had a risk tolerance adjustment. Their new investment objective became: sell everything now before it was too late!

That day left an impression on me that defined my career, as I realized that markets will produce events that were well beyond what most investors, advisors and the financial advice industry itself would view as a worst case scenario. The mental and emotional strain these events place on some people results in their making decisions that would never be expected to come from rational individuals.

I was fortunate, since my retirement planning clients had diversified portfolios. Despite having a clientele that was essentially intact, I realized that the financial industry was changing dramatically. The profitability of brokerage firms was trampled as the events of Black Monday were now ingrained in the minds of investors. They used new market rallies to sell and then remove funds from equities, or they just simply stopped trading. Brokerage firms were retrenching and the Canadian banks seized on this opportunity to begin purchasing the independent brokerage firms. As client commission revenues decreased, brokers in my office either began leaving or were asked to leave. Many left the industry permanently.

A call from a head hunter in 1989 convinced me to make a career change to the trust industry. I was just recently married and my wife and I wanted to start a family, so I wasn't entirely comfortable with the monthly ups and downs of a purely commission driven sales career. I also believed that, with the banks owning the brokerage firms, they were soon going to change the industry to suit their needs and the likely result would be a reduction in autonomy for brokerage firm employees. The trust industry was still independent from the banks and was generally viewed at that time as being more progressive in providing financial services for individuals.

When I resigned my job as a broker, I was one of seven advisors who were still left in my office, down from a peak of twenty only four years earlier.

My trust industry career allowed me to gain experience in off-shore investing, estate and trust planning, and helped me further my investment career. The trust companies had large money management divisions that looked after investment assets in trust and estate accounts. Managing money for clients was my ultimate career goal, without having the additional burden of making a sale as a reason to complete a trade.

I spent eight years in the trust industry, with the last six as a discretionary portfolio manager. I also continued my education by completing the requirements to obtain the Chartered Financial Analyst designation. The trust industry eventually followed the same fate as the independent brokerage firms, as the Canadian banks consolidated their hold on the financial services industry by eventually purchasing the trust companies. Bank ownership changed how money was managed in the trust divisions. Initially, portfolio managers had the autonomy to select individual securities from approved lists, which were created through research performed by analysts employed by the trust companies. Bank ownership removed that autonomy by introducing the use of internal pooled funds as the only investment alternatives for portfolio managers. The pooled funds were simply different versions of the bank's retail mutual fund offerings, with the internal management fees removed. The fees were instead charged directly to the trust accounts, but at a lower scale than what the retail mutual fund investors would pay.

Unfortunately, many of the pooled funds, even with the fee reduction, were unable to provide better performance than the returns of the comparable financial market indexes that were used as benchmarks on client statements. In many cases the returns were substantially lower than index returns. It was at this time that I became convinced that index investing (investing directly in a financial market index) versus active investing (selecting securities that are projected to have a better return than the index benchmark) was a superior investment alternative for individual investors.

The financial advice industry still makes a very large amount of money by convincing individual investors that they should pursue an active approach to managing their investment assets. The higher fees that these products charge pay the salaries of the analysts, economists and sales people that are employed throughout the financial advice industry. You are correct if this appears to be a self-serving process.

Successfully navigating your way through financial markets and the financial advice industry can be a daunting task. If you have made investment decisions, then you will have also discovered that the results you expect are not always what occur. Even with experience and knowledge, you will often make investment decisions that leave you disappointed.

Is there a better way to align your investment results with your expectations? I believe that there is, and it begins by examining why you make the wrong decisions. This book will provide you with a better understanding of how improving your decision making can steer you toward investment success.

CHAPTER 1

NEURONS, ELECTROCHEMICALS AND WATER

"If the brain were so simple we could understand it, we would be so simple we couldn't."

Lyall Watson, biologist and author

The average human brain weighs 1300 grams, is 167 mm in length, 140 mm in width and 93 mm in height. It contains 100 billion neurons, yet is composed 78% of water. [1]

Neurons are cells that process and transmit information by electrochemical signaling. Neurons are the core components of the brain, spinal cord and peripheral nerves located on your body. You also use sensory neurons that respond to touch, sound, light and numerous other stimuli that communicate their presence to the central nervous system. The nervous system processes the information and sends the responses to other parts your body so you can take the appropriate action. The transmitting of electrochemical signals is estimated to require only tens of milliseconds. This means that in a period of just one second, your brain produces millions of signals.

You use your brain to navigate your world, yet how can it be possible for rational decisions to arise out of matter that is composed primarily of water and uses electro-chemical signals that transmit at almost instantaneous speed?

What Is Thought?

Cognition is the scientific term for the *process of thought*. The term refers to a faculty for the processing of information, applying knowledge and changing preferences. Cognitive processes can be natural or artificial, conscious or unconscious.[2]

You mostly view your cognitive processes as deliberate, clear and logical. You will consider all the relevant stimulus inputs, hold a great number of facts in your memory, use your *mind's eye* to view the results of your potential actions, develop reliable inferences that allow you to evaluate the pros and cons of these different actions on immediate and future goals, and then make a decision for the best possible outcomes across all time horizons.

But is this the only way that you think?

Think Fast!

We have all had the experience of seeing an object out of the corner of your eye that is speeding toward you, so you duck quickly to avoid getting hit.

This is a situation that requires an almost instantaneous response, but to select the appropriate response you do not use a conscious reasoning process. The information you required to act was initially part of a conscious process when you learned for the first time that getting hit by flying objects hurts, so ducking to avoid them is a better outcome than being hit. This previous experience made your brain establish a strong link between the stimulus input (seeing a flying object) and the best possible outcome (ducking to avoid getting hit).

Your response to an object flying toward you now comes from your previous strong link between the stimulus and the response, which produces an automatic or rapid response without requiring a deliberate logical reasoning process.

Being of Two Minds

Recent studies of our brains and the how our thought processes work, have concluded that there actually is a neurological basis for the phrase *being of two minds* and that both these minds compete for dominance when we make decisions.[3]

As we have developed as a species, so has our brain. As our environment has grown more complex and required new decision making strategies, evolutionary development has not only enhanced our cognitive processes, but also retained links to our primal brain functions that focus on such basic things as our well-being, pleasure and pain.

Therefore, being of two minds can refer to our evolved *logical brain* and our primal *automatic brain*.[4]

The logical brain is deliberate and coherent. It allows you to solve a math equation. The automatic brain is instinctive and reactive. It pulls your hand away quickly when you touch a hot stove.

The automatic brain allows you to avoid risks as quickly as possible and will often respond to a stimulus before the logical brain even realizes that there is anything you need to respond to. It acts as an initial filter for the stimulus that you encounter. Once a stimulus is detected, the automatic brain works to quickly evaluate not only the risks, but also the rewards. Your reactions to these evaluations can be either basic emotions, like fear and pleasure, or a more complex reaction involving some social behaviour that helps you determine how you should react.

Therefore, you have two ways to think and they are both linked. This contrasts with how most individuals believe they think and make decisions by using only their logical brain to always produce responses to new information. Intuitively this makes sense, because we view ourselves as being rational intelligent beings. However, when you read the scenario below, it's clear that your thought process is much more complex.

Closing the Deal

Let me introduce Jerry. Jerry is a likeable fellow who is a salesperson for Sales Are Us Inc. Through his hard work over the past several years, Jerry has developed a reputation with the firm's management as an excellent employee. He has consistently met all his quarterly sales targets and his supervisor has just told him that if he can meet his next sales threshold he will not only receive a substantial bonus, but will also be considered for a promotion to manage his own sales staff for a new corporate subsidiary.

Through his marketing efforts, he has finally booked a meeting with Mr. Big, a new prospective client who is currently dealing with the largest competitor to Sales Are Us Inc. In his meeting, Jerry discovers that both he and Mr. Big have a mutual acquaintance in Bernie. Bernie is the salesperson that Mr. Big is currently dealing with at the competitor, but he is also a close friend of Jerry's. In fact, Mr. Big is Bernie's largest client. Jerry also knows that Bernie is just about to sign a contract to build a new house, because he told Jerry that his sales income is now finally large enough that he can make the house purchase after years of working toward this goal.

This scenario obviously calls for a choice to be made. Jerry's brain will soon begin an analyzing process by creating scenarios of possible responses and their expected outcomes. In his mind's eye, these scenarios are similar to a series of flash card images that will appear. These images could include: receiving his bonus; telling his family about his new promotion; imagining Bernie explaining to his supervisor that he lost his largest client; or explaining to his family that they will not be building a new house after all.

The Battle of the Minds

Now imagine yourself with Jerry's dilemma. If you only use your logical brain to analyze the possible outcomes of your actions, then you must remove all emotions from your analysis. You must look at each possible choice you could make, and think solely about the advantages and disadvantages of each outcome at every point in the future: You can gain a new client that will bring you a bonus and a promotion, but you will likely harm your friend financially. Is money more important than his friendship? Will there ever be a future client as large as Mr. Big? What will happen to your future income if you let this opportunity pass by? Will you ever get another opportunity for a promotion? How angry will your friend be with you for taking his largest client? Will he be angry enough to end your friendship? How will his family react?

Now ask yourself if you could really answer these questions without feeling a sense of worry, dread, excitement, greed or fear?

This analysis can get increasingly complex because not only will you have to evaluate these questions and many others similar to them, but also how the answers to the questions may change in the future. Will your friend's anger subside as time passes, or will it remain the same?

You need to evaluate all these potential outcomes and somehow make them comparable, so that you can then make a logical choice for the best decision.

If you only use your logical brain, it is likely that your decision timeframe on what course of action to take will be excruciatingly long. You may not be able to even make a decision, because the various scenarios you have in your mind's eye will lead to others; that will lead to others and will continue in an almost endless series.

Now imagine yourself in Jerry's place once again, but now with your automatic brain allowed to be involved in the decision making process. When the possible outcomes of your potential actions appear in your mind's eye and even before you can evaluate the various advantages and disadvantages, you will experience a *feeling* or, as it is often referred to, a *gut feeling*.

What does this feeling accomplish? It draws the attention of your logical brain to an outcome and then allows you to either immediately reject the outcome, in the case of a bad feeling or, in the case of a good feeling, allow that outcome to be a benchmark against which other projected outcomes are now compared. The result is that your logical brain now has to choose between fewer alternatives. The decision process is then narrowed so that the decision timeframe will be lessened. Your logical brain still performs its evaluation, but it uses a *shortcut* from your automatic brain to increase the efficiency of the decision making process.

So, the dynamic duo of your automatic and logical brains will always allow you to evaluate your world by processing information efficiently to then make rational decisions.

If it were only this simple...

The Gambling Experiment

A gambling experiment (Bechara et al 1994) was conducted in which a player sits in front of four decks of cards labelled A, B, C and D. The player is then given a loan of $2000 in authentic looking play money and is told that the goal of the game is twofold:[5]

- Try not to lose money,

- But also try to make as much money as possible.

The game progresses by turning cards one at a time from any of the four decks until the person in charge of the experiment says to stop. Therefore, the player does not know the total number of turns before the game will end. The player is also told that turning each card will always result in earning a sum of money but, every now and then, turning a card will require that some amount of money must be paid back to the person in charge of the experiment.

The amount of gain or loss on any card, a card's connection to a specific deck, and the order of any card's appearance is not disclosed before the game begins. Instead, the amount to be earned or paid by a card is disclosed only after it is turned. No other instruction is provided. The tally of how much is earned or lost at any point in the game as it progresses is not disclosed and the player is not allowed to keep written notes.

The decks are stacked so that turning the cards in decks A and B pays $100, while turning the cards in decks C and D only pays $50. However, cards in both of the $100 paying decks can also require an unpredictable repayment of a large amount, up to $1,250. Likewise, certain cards in the $50 paying decks also require an unpredictable repayment, but the sums are smaller, being less than $50 on average.

The rules of the game are never changed and, unbeknownst to the player, the game ends after 100 card turns. There is no way for the player to predict at the outset what will happen and they are not provided with any calculation tools that can be used to maintain a precise tally of the gains and losses as the game proceeds.

The game structure is similar to what occurs in many situations in your own life. Much of the information you receive to make your decisions only becomes available to you in small increments. Until you develop some experience in a particular situation, uncertainty will reign. Your knowledge, like that of the game player, is shaped by the environment you find yourself in, and your responses are shaped by your beliefs, preferences and goals.

Most participants played the game by sampling from all four decks, in search of patterns and clues. More often than not, they are initially lured by the experience of receiving high rewards from turning cards in the $100 decks. However, within the first thirty moves, they switch their preference to the $50 decks. They would then generally stick to this strategy until the end of the game. Self-professed aggressive players occasionally sample from the $100 decks later in the game, only to return eventually to the more prudent course of action of continuing to select mainly from the $50 decks.

Since there is no way for players to carry out a precise prediction of the gains and losses, they gradually develop a hunch that the $100 decks are more *risky* than the others. They perceive that the lower penalties in the $50 decks may allow them to come out ahead in the long run, despite the smaller initial gains. The researchers who conducted the experiment believed that what was occurring beneath this conscious hunch (think: the logical brain), is an unconscious process (think: the automatic brain) that is gradually formulating a prediction for the outcome of each move. The unconscious process alerts the player with increasing intensity that punishment or reward is about to occur if a certain move is carried out. The researchers concluded that this is neither a fully conscious process (think: logical brain only), nor fully unconscious process (think: automatic brain only), but it instead takes both types of processing for the brain to operate in this experiment.[6]

When I first came across this experiment many years ago, it struck me that, although the experiment was used to evaluate how gambling decisions are made, it also had many striking similarities to how I observed individual investors behaving when they made decisions in financial markets.

Remember the observations the researcher made during the experiment:

"The goal of the game is to not lose money, but to try and make as much money as possible"

The primary investment goal of most individual investors is to make money and avoid losses.

"The amount to be earned or paid by a given card is disclosed only after a card is turned"

The prices of most investments will fluctuate but an investor does not know in advance whether the next price change will be up or down, or how large the change will be.

"Cards that produce gains are interspersed with other cards that result in large unpredictable losses"

Many investments are subject to unpredictable price changes that can result in large losses.

"There is no way for the player to predict at the outset what will happen"

Most types of investments do not allow an individual investor to predict the precise outcome of the investment return in advance when they make the initial decision.

"Most people play the game by sampling from all four decks, in search of patterns and clues".

Most investors gain experience in how financial markets operate by initially making investments in one class of securities and, when they gain confidence in that outcome, they sample another class of securities.

"More often than not, lured by the experience of high rewards from turning cards in the $100 decks, they show an early preference for those decks."

Most individual investors gain their early investment experience by beginning with higher risk investments (think: one-stock portfolios).

"Players perceive that the lower penalties in $50 decks may make them come out ahead in the long run, despite the smaller initial gains."

As individual investors learn from their investment experiences, many change their investments to a more conservative approach (think: diversified portfolios).

"Self-professed aggressive players occasionally sample from the $100 decks, only to return later to the more prudent course of action".

Individual investors each have a unique engrained tolerance for risk that is affected by their changing perceptions of the relevance of new information.

Despite what individual investors and many financial advisors believe, both your logical and automatic brains are constantly involved in your investment decision making processes. Unfortunately, the dynamic duo of your two brains does not always serve you well.

CHAPTER 2

YOUR INVESTING BRAIN

*"Whenever stress rises, the human brain switches to autopilot and has
an inherent tendency to do more of the same, only harder. This, more
often than not, is precisely the wrong approach in today's world".*

Dr. Robert K. Cooper, researcher and author

The fundamental assumption of investment decision making is grounded in the belief that when individual investors are faced with uncertainty, they will rationally and intentionally search between alternatives, make an impartial prediction of the future and then make a choice that leads to the highest possible financial gain.

Is this assumption correct? Do you always process information so that your logical and automatic brains allow you to consistently make optimal decisions?

Look at the set of lines below. Which one is longer?

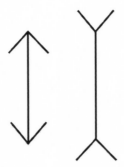

If you are like most people, you will choose the line on the right, but both lines are the same length. Even if you have seen this illusion previously, you will still struggle to accept the correct answer.

The illusion was developed by a German psychiatrist named Franz Müller-Lyer in 1889, yet it is still effective today. The orientation of the arrowheads affects your ability to accurately perceive the length of the lines. The illusion fools us by appealing to the automatic brain rather than the logical brain.[7]

You need both parts of your brain to analyze information, but how these parts function together can also lead to systematic errors and biases, especially when you need to make financial decisions.

I discussed earlier that our brain uses shortcuts as a way to process information quickly, which then allow us to make judgments so that we don't spend all day analyzing.

Although these shortcuts are sensible, they are formed through memories and mental associations. These associations trigger emotions that also influence your interpretation of the information you are processing. Decisions that you make during periods of uncertainty magnify your underlying emotions, which creates information processing biases.[8]

You are biased by not only how you process information, but also by the way you *feel* about the information when you are processing it.

There are two expanding bodies of scientific research that are now studying how individual investors make decisions and how behavioural and emotional factors affect these decisions.

Neuroeconomics combines psychology, economics and neuroscience to study how individuals make decisions. It looks at the functioning of our brain when we make evaluation decisions to judge risks and rewards.

Behavioural economics and its related area of study, behavioural finance, use social, cognitive and emotional factors in understanding the investment decisions of investors and their effects on market prices and investment returns. The goal is to learn how the behaviour of individuals in financial settings differs from that which is perceived to be rational behaviour.

These fields of study have identified numerous biases that result in the patterns of decision making by individual investors being systematically different from what we would consider to be rational.

Shortcuts to Ruin

Heuristics are experience-based mental processes by which you evaluate possible answers and solve problems. This usually occurs by a process of trial and error (think: the gambling experiment).

Heuristics lead to the shortcuts or *rules of thumb,* which you use to draw inferences and make decisions from the information you receive. In many circumstances, these shortcuts are close to being correct, but they also frequently result in some decisions being repetitively wrong. The result is that you are susceptible to particular types of errors because of your *heuristic biases*.

The most common heuristic biases are described below. Can you see your own thoughts and actions in these descriptions?

Availability Bias – "Trade the News"

You will predict the frequency of an event, based on how easily the occurrence of a previous similar event can be remembered. If you can remember it quickly, then you believe that it must be important. Therefore, recent events tend to have a greater impact on your decisions than past events and, consequently, recent news is viewed as more important than previous news. [9]

Most individual investors rely on some type of media reports for a large amount of the information they receive regarding financial markets and investments. The financial media tends to report some types of information frequently because they view it as newsworthy.

Individuals who succumb to availability heuristic will view the more frequently reported information as important and allow it to influence their investment decision making, rather than objectively weighing its relevance.

CNBC is a widely viewed cable television network that reports on business news and provides live coverage of financial markets. The combined reach of CNBC and its affiliates is 390 million viewers around the world. [10]

CNBC broadcasts a time clock countdown on your television screen prior to the scheduled release of many U.S. Government economic statistics. The countdown usually starts thirty minutes to one hour prior to the announcement time. The moment the statistic is released, the result is flashed across your television screen as breaking news and read with great excitement by a network news personality. The perception of urgency and importance that surrounds this type of media tactic, appeals directly to the availability bias of individual investors.

Availability bias can also influence your perception of risk, or that the likelihood of an investment outcome will be favourable. Many individual investors will imagine what the potential outcome of an investment may be prior to making their decision to invest. Frequently the image in your mind's eye is a positive outcome that provides you with a financial reward. Studies have shown that when you are asked to view an outcome in a positive way, you are then much more likely to believe that this outcome is likely to occur. This happens since a recent mental image is more easily recalled than a past image, so the recent image seems more relevant and is then more influential in your decision making process.[11]

Have you ever dreamed of winning a lottery and then purchased a ticket because you felt you were going to win? Did you believe that purchasing the ticket didn't seem like you were wasting your money because you had the dream about winning? Did your dream come true?

Representativeness Bias – "I Will Wait For a Correction to Buy"

You will often make judgments by relying on stereotypes. While this process may be correct in some circumstances, it can be very misleading in others. In many situations, it can result in you violating one of the fundamental properties of probability.

Imagine that you are being told for the first time about your wife's new friend Linda.

Linda is 31 years old, single, outspoken and very bright. In university, she majored in philosophy. As a student, she was deeply concerned with issues of discrimination and social justice, and she also participated in public demonstrations related to global environmental sustainability. Which of these two alternatives is more probable?

(a) Linda is a bank teller;

(b) Linda is a bank teller and is active in the feminist movement.

If you are like most people you chose (b), even though it is the less likely choice. How is it less likely? Because the conjunction of two events (Linda is a bank teller and active in the feminist movement) is less likely than her simply being a bank teller, regardless of her political interests. The probability that two events will both occur cannot ever be greater than the probability that each event will occur individually.

Daniel Kahneman and Amos Tversky created the now famous *Linda problem* as an example of representativeness. Kahneman and Tversky were early pioneers in the discovery of systematic heuristic biases and have completed numerous studies that I will cite throughout this book.

Imagine that you purchase a stock and then watch its price increase for 10 consecutive trading days. What should you do: sell or hold?

You may believe that you should sell the stock since it cannot possibly rise in price for an 11th consecutive day. Or can it?

Imagine that you purchase a stock and then watch its price decline for 10 consecutive trading days. What should you do: sell or hold?

You may believe that you should continue to hold the stock; since it has fallen for so many days in a row any further decline is unlikely. Or is it?

In both these regularly occurring financial market scenarios, representativeness bias is present and has an influence on your investment decision making process. The fact that a stock has advanced or declined in any previous trading session does not have any bearing on whether it is more likely to reverse direction during the next trading session. Although you should know that this fact is correct, you struggle to overcome the influence of the past on your decisions about tomorrow.

Affect Bias – "Goodness vs. Badness"

Your automatic brain produces feelings, such as fear, pleasure or surprise. These responses occur rapidly and involuntarily when you encounter a stimulus, and are not part of your logical thought process.

Affect is a specific quality of *goodness* or *badness* that you experience as a feeling, when separating the positive or negative quality of a stimulus you encounter.[12]

When you see the words *hate, treasure, winner* and *cancer*, what feelings do you experience?

If your feelings are pleasant, they tend to motivate actions and thoughts that are intended to reproduce the same feelings. If your feelings are unpleasant, they tend to motivate actions and thoughts that are intended to avoid the same feelings.

All of the images stored in your memory that are recalled by your mind's eye, have been attached or tagged to varying degrees with affect. You consult or *sense* the effect on these images in the process of making judgments. For this reason, the affect heuristic is a close cousin of representativeness.

Affect is widely understood and used in the marketing techniques for consumer products, such as cars (think: BMW vs. Hyundai) and watches (think: Rolex vs. Timex) and it also plays a role in shaping your investment decisions. Consider names like Apple or Google, which are currently consumer brand leaders. You can form a positive impression of a stock before you consider the merits of the investment based solely on financial facts. The result is that corporations who currently sell well-regarded consumer products may also tend to have share prices that frequently trade at excessive financial valuations.

Studies have also shown that there is evidence that sunny weather is associated with a positive effect on individuals. Morning sunshine is associated with positive daily stock returns, so perhaps you should check the weather forecast before you make your investment decisions. [13]

Affect also has an influence on risk perception. Although risk and return tend to be positively correlated (think: a direct association), studies of risk perception have found that they are negatively correlated in your mind's eye and in your judgments. There is an inverse relationship between the perceived risk and perceived reward of an activity that is also linked to the strength of the positive or negative affect associated with that activity. [14]

If your feeling from a stimulus is favourable, then you tend to judge the risk as low and the benefit as large; conversely, if your feelings from the stimulus are unfavourable, then you tend to judge the risk as large and the benefit as low. Studies have shown that feelings of dread were the major determiner of public perception and acceptance of risk for a wide range of hazards. [15]

Do you remember the era of the dot com companies that dominated market returns for a short period during the early 2000s? Affect frequently led to the share prices of these well-regarded corporations (think: Nortel Networks) trading at excessive financial valuations and it also resulted in them being perceived as less risky. Is it any surprise that these types of investments eventually disappoint individual investors?

Overconfidence Bias – "I Always Make Money"

You tend to hold overly favourable views of your own abilities. As a result, you are overconfident in the reliability of your own judgments to a much greater degree than should be expected based on facts alone. For this reason, you tend to be surprised by an outcome more frequently than you would anticipate.

We all tend to think that we are better than our peers. In survey responses individuals consistently rate themselves as being above average when they are asked to compare their abilities to a group. Being overconfident is not necessarily a bad personality trait, as it can boost your self-esteem and give you courage to try new things. However, the drawback is that it also leads to overestimating your chances of success or underestimating risks. It leads you to believe that you can control or influence outcomes, when in reality you cannot.

Studies have shown (Barber and Odean 1999) that overconfidence is a major contributing factor toward overtrading by individual investors, which results in higher transactional costs that decrease the return of a portfolio. Overconfidence causes individual investors to become too assured about their own judgments and not adequately consider the opinions of others. This false belief in your superior judgment is also linked to a perception that your investment decisions are less volatile and risky than is actually the case.[16]

You tend to be optimistic and even unrealistic in your belief about your future prospects. You are also inclined to rate your future success as being more favourable than that of your peers. In a 2001 Gallup/Paine Webber survey, individual investors predicted that the average stock market return for the next year would be 10.30%, but they expected the average return of their own portfolio would be 11.70%.[17]

As I will discuss later in this book, the likelihood of achieving investment performance that exceeds the return of a market index is an extremely elusive goal for individual investors.

Hindsight Bias – "I Knew It Would Double!"

You are inclined to see events that have already occurred as being more predictable than they actually were before they took place. You also tend to remember your predictions of future events as having been more accurate than they were in reality, especially in the cases where those predictions turn out to be correct.

Once you learn what occurred, you look back and believe that you knew all along that the result was going to happen. This encourages individual investors to view financial markets as being more predictable than they actually are.

Hindsight bias develops as you detect new information. Your brain immediately processes the information by incorporating it into what you already understand. This revised understanding then becomes the benchmark from which future information will be evaluated. This process limits your ability to go back in time to objectively assess your state of knowledge at the precise moment that a past event occurred.

In October 1987, Robert Shiller conducted research using questionnaire surveys to learn about investor behaviour as part of a project at Yale University. The timing of this study was unique because on Monday October 19th, 1987 world equity markets had just experienced the largest single day declines in financial market history. As an example, the Dow Jones Industrial Average declined 508 points or 22%.[18]

The questionnaire was sent to individual investors by 5:00 pm on October 21st, so that it was received while their memories were still fresh. The questionnaire required them to write their own answers to provoke thoughtful responses.

One of the questions was aimed at discovering what investors thought on October 19th by asking "Did they *know* when a rebound would occur?" Answers from 29.2% of the respondents stated that they did indeed know a rebound would occur.

Respondents were then asked "If yes, what made you think you knew a rebound would occur?" Frequent answers were: "intuition", "gut feeling" or "I just knew that there would be a rebound".

If 29.2% of the respondents really did know a rebound would occur, it would be rational to believe that they would have acted on that knowledge. After all, the profit potential would have been enormous after such a large decline in prices. However, the number of individuals who indicated that they *knew* of a future recovery was actually ten times greater than the number who indicated elsewhere in the survey that they actually purchased stocks that day. Shiller commented, "Many investors believe that they have some internal sense of magnitude or direction for the market."

The survey results indicated that many individuals were emotionally involved in the market (think: automatic brain). The survey asked about actual symptoms of anxiety experienced by respondents. The answers revealed that 20.3% had difficulty concentrating, sweaty palms, tightness in their chest and a rapid pulse, which are each tell-tale signs of emotional stress.

Money Illusion – "A Dollar Today > A Dollar Tomorrow"

Money illusion refers to the tendency of individual investors to think of investment returns only in terms of nominal value. The term was coined by the economist John Maynard Keynes in his early twentieth century writings.

Nominal value only uses current market value without taking into account the past and future effects that inflation has on the purchasing power of an investment. The alternative is to use *real* value, which is the value after accounting for the effects of inflation.

Imagine you purchase a bond for $100 that pays an annual 5% rate of interest. You begin the year with $100 and will finish the year with $105. However, the $5, or 5%, you received is the nominal interest rate and does not account for the effects of inflation. Whenever interest rates are quoted, they refer to the nominal rate of interest, unless it is stated otherwise.

If the inflation rate was 3% for that year, then a $100 item that you could purchase at the beginning of the year would cost $103 by the end of the year. If you take into account the effects of inflation, then the $100 bond has earned a real return of only 2%.

Money illusion can influence your perception of which outcome is most beneficial to select. You will tend to choose a 4% nominal investment return in an environment of 2% inflation, over a 2% real investment return, even though the real returns of the two alternatives are equivalent. You believe that the 4% quoted interest rate has to be more attractive because it appears to be greater.

A dollar today is worth more than a dollar tomorrow and they are both worth much more than the value of a dollar in forty years. Inflation erodes the future purchasing power of your investments. This erosion is deceiving to most individual investors because it occurs slowly and compounds over time.

A proxy for the rate of inflation in Canada is shown by the monthly price change in the consumer price index (CPI). This index calculates changes in the cost of a fixed basket of consumer items that includes food, shelter, furniture, clothing, transportation and recreation.

In the forty year period from 1970 to 2010 the average annual inflation rate was 4.45%. A $100 investment in 1970 had to increase to $570 by 2010 just to maintain the same real value.[19]

You need to overcome the effects of money illusion in order to understand how inflation affects the real purchasing power of your investments over long time horizons.

The Fed Illusion

The 1978 Humphrey Hawkins Full Employment Act requires that the U.S. Federal Reserve Open Market Committee report to Congress on the economy and monetary policy twice each year. These reports are carefully scrutinized by investment analysts and the financial media. Contained in the July 22, 1997 report was the following comment:

"The ratio of prices in the S&P 500 to consensus estimates of earnings over the coming twelve months has risen further from levels that were already unusually high. Changes in this ratio have often been inversely related to changes in long-term Treasury yields, but this year's stock price gains were not matched by a significant net decline in interest rates. As a result, the yield on 10-year Treasury notes now exceeds the ratio of twelve-month-ahead earnings to prices by the largest amount since 1991, when earnings were depressed by the economic slowdown."[20]

This comment was immediately pounced upon by financial market participants, as acceptance that the Federal Reserve was using an equity market valuation model that compared the market's earnings yield (think: earnings/price, which is the inverse of the well-known price/earnings ratio) to long-term treasury yields (think: current nominal interest rates). This ratio quickly became known as the *Fed Model*, despite the fact that the Federal Reserve never formally endorsed its validity as a valuation tool, nor has any mention of it ever been made again in any subsequent communications.

There is an appealing premise to the model that is based on a theory of competition among asset classes for investment dollars: as bond interest rates increase they become more attractive, which means more competition for equities, and this should be reflected in equity valuations.

The concept seems reasonable, but unfortunately the model succumbs to money illusion. The earnings yield on stocks is an estimate of the expected *real* return on stocks. It is *not* an estimate of the expected *nominal* return on stocks. For the earnings yield to move in a perfect positive correlation with nominal bond yields, then you have to believe that the *nominal* yield on bonds equals the *real* return on stocks.

The Fed Model is not an accurate forecasting tool, since there is not a constant positive correlation between earnings yields for U.S. equities and Treasury note interest rates in long-term historical data. Market history has shown that when P/E ratios are high, expected future stock returns are low and vice versa, regardless of the level of nominal interest rates.[21]

Herding – "When Are Hotdogs like Stocks?"

Herding refers to the phenomenon of how individuals, who are acting independently, can sometimes unintentionally act together as a group.

Herding behaviours are common in your everyday decisions. Imagine you are walking down the street and you approach two hot dog vendors. Neither has a line of people waiting to order, so at random you choose one of the vendors. Soon another two individuals stroll down the street in search of a place to eat and they see you at one vendor, while the other vendor still does not have a customer. On the assumption that having customers makes one vendor a better choice, they join the line with you. Another passerby sees that one vendor is doing more business than the other, processes the same information and then joins the growing line, while the other vendor sits idle.

Financial market history is littered with examples of investments that begin as new ideas, then become fads, which turn into bubbles and inevitably into busts: tulip mania in Holland in the 17th century, the South Sea Island bubble of the 18th century, the U.S. stock market boom of the 1920s, the internet and technology investment boom of the early 2000s and, more recently, the residential real estate bubble that occurred in many developed economies in the late 2000s. These episodes are often cited as examples of herding behaviour.[22]

In many financial market environments individual investors are influenced by the decisions of other investors, resulting in them all herding towards the same investments.

Suppose that 100 potential investors each make their own independent judgments about the potential profitability of investing in a particular stock. Only 20 of the investors believe that this is likely to be a profitable investment at the current price, while the other 80 believe that it is not worthwhile.

This is the same type of environment in which real financial markets function, as buyers and sellers of securities always having differing opinions regarding the same security. When you want to purchase a stock, someone must be willing to sell it.

Each investor is the only one who knows their own estimate of the profitability of an investment. They have no way of ascertaining the judgments of the other investors or whether a majority have decided to purchase the stock. However, if these investors did share their knowledge about the estimate of the potential profitability of investment, they would collectively decide that investing in the stock is not a good idea (80 'against' vs. 20 'for').

Imagine that these 100 investors do not all make their investment decisions at exactly the same moment. Instead, the first few investors that decide to act are the 20 investors who believe that this will be a profitable investment, and so they purchase the stock. Several of the investors who choose not to invest in the stock notice the increase in the buying activity and the resulting increase in the price of the stock, so they reverse their original decision and also purchase the stock, thinking that there must have been something wrong with their original opinion of value. In turn, this begins a cascading effect that results in most of the remaining individuals reversing their original decisions and now purchasing the stock as they use the same flawed decision-making process (think: representativeness).

Once all the investors have finished purchasing the stock, the buying volume is finished and the price begins to decline. Some of the original 20 investors that purchased the stock early have made a profit, so they begin to sell. Other investors notice the change of direction in the stock price and they join the sellers.

Herd behaviour that can arise from informational differences:

- The actions and judgments of investors that appear early can be crucial in determining which way the majority will decide.

- The decision that investors herd on may well be incorrect.

- After investors make a decision, then with experience or the arrival of new information, they can eventually reverse their decision, starting a herd in the opposite direction.

When you join a crowd of other individual investors in a rush to get in or out of markets, it's the result of your automatic brain (think: greed in the bubbles, fear in the busts) overriding your logical brain. Herd behaviour has the potential to increase financial market volatility.

Risk & Loss Aversion – "That Stock Will Come Back"

Risk aversion refers to an individual investor's preference to choose an investment with a more certain, but possibly lower, expected outcome compared to an investment with an uncertain outcome. Individuals often choose investments with low but guaranteed interest rates, rather than investments that have the potential for higher returns, which also come with the chance of declining below the initial purchase cost.

Loss aversion results from the preference of most individuals to strongly prefer avoiding losses to acquiring gains. This phenomenon was first demonstrated in studies by Tversky and Kahneman. The studies suggested that your brain evaluates the emotional impact of losses and gains differently, with losses producing an impact that is more powerful than gains. Consequently, when multiple gain and loss events happen, each event is valued separately and then combined to create a cumulative feeling.

Imagine that you have the good fortune of finding $50 on the sidewalk. You place the bill into your pocket and walk to a store that is located in the next block. Once inside the store, you reach into your pocket to pay for a purchase and discover that the bill is gone. Somehow it fell out of your pocket. How would you feel?

Chances are that you would berate yourself over losing the found $50, because the loss has a more powerful feeling even though the true economic impact to you is $0.

The graph below illustrates this loss aversion effect:

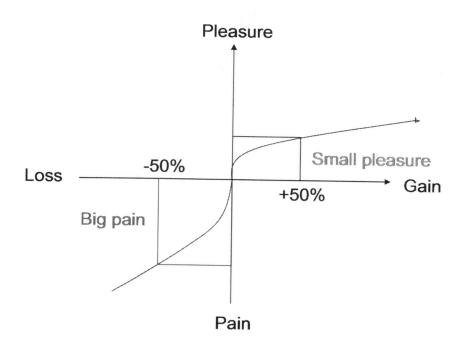

Loss aversion explains the reluctance of individual investors to sell investments that will result in a loss.

Imagine that within your investment account you purchase two securities. If you are like most investors, these initial purchase costs will now become your continuing reference points for the success of your investment decisions. One security appreciates and one security declines. You now need to make a withdrawal from the account, so you will have to sell one security to raise the funds. You do not have any new information about either security that may influence your opinion of the future prices of the two securities. Which one would you sell?

Most individual investors would choose to sell the security with the gain, even though the transaction will produce a capital gain that will require a future tax payment. The most rational decision would be to sell the security with the loss, since no tax would be owed and the capital loss can be carried forward indefinitely for tax purposes.

A study by Odean (1998) confirmed the tendency of individual investors to hold losing investments too long and sell winning investments too soon. The study analyzed trading account records for 10,000 investors at a discount brokerage firm. Throughout the study, investors' reference points were assumed to be their purchase prices. These investors demonstrated a strong preference for selling winners rather than losers.[23]

Prospect Theory

Prospect Theory explains this tendency for individual investors to hold on to losing stocks and sell winning stocks.

The theory was developed by Kahneman and Tversky in 1979 and resulted in the researchers being awarded the Nobel Prize in economics in 2002. The theory describes how individuals make choices in circumstances where they have to decide between alternatives that involve risk.

The theory builds on the basis of risk and loss aversion, by which individuals value gains and losses differently, and shows that individuals also base their decisions on perceived gains rather than perceived losses. As a result, if you are given two equal choices, one expressed in terms of possible gains and the other in possible losses, you will choose the former, even if it provides the same monetary result.

Individuals tend to decide between which outcomes they see as basically identical, and then set these outcomes as reference points from which they consider lower outcomes as losses and larger ones as gains.

Consider an example where you are presented with $10,000 and then given two choices:

The first choice involves accepting a sure loss of $7500.

The second choice involves accepting a bet that has a 75% chance you will lose $10,000 or a 25% chance you will lose nothing.

Which choice would you prefer?

The probability outcome of both choices is a loss $7500, but most individuals select the second choice. Why? Because they do not like the feeling of losing and the second choice offers a chance that they won't have to experience the emotional pain of a loss.

The implication of Prospect Theory is that individual investors do not assess risky choices following the principals of rationality. Rather, in assessing such choices, they do not focus on the levels of the final wealth they can attain, but instead view gains and losses relative to some reference point, which may vary from situation to situation.

To the detriment of individual investors, they are willing to assume a higher level of risk in order to avoid the emotional pain of loss. Unfortunately, many securities decline for valid reasons and never recover in price, so there is frequently a financial price to pay for not wanting to feel regret.

Frames – "Half Full or Half Empty?"

Imagine that I am holding a glass that is partially filled with water. Is it half full or half empty? Either answer is acceptable because they can both be perceived as being correct.

I am still holding the same glass that is partially filled with water, but I now tell you I just drank some of it. Is it half full or half empty? Most individuals will now answer the question with *half empty* because they have a mind's eye picture of me drinking some of the water.

I am still holding the same glass that is still partially filled with water, but I now tell you I just filled it from the faucet. Is it half full or half empty? Most people will now answer the question with *half full* because they have a mind's eye picture of me adding some of the water.

Framing refers to how the way in which information is presented can influence your decisions. As a result, the choices that you make are influenced significantly by the way your problems are framed.

Framing decision problems in a positive way generally results in less risky choices. While negative framing of problems tends to result in riskier choices.

The most widely cited study of decision framing was called the Asian Disease and was completed by Tversky and Kahneman (1981). It demonstrated that individuals system-atically reverse their choices when the same problem was presented in different ways.[24]

In the study, participants were asked to imagine that the U.S. is preparing for the outbreak of an unusual Asian disease, which is expected to kill 600 people. Two alternative programs to combat the disease have been proposed.

The first group of participants were presented with a choice between two programs:

- Program A: "200 people will be saved"

- Program B: "there is a one-third probability that 600 people will be saved, and a two-thirds probability that no one will be saved"

After reviewing the choices, 72% of participants preferred program A. The remaining 28% opted for program B.

The second groups of participants were presented with the choice between:

- Program C: "400 people will die"

- Program D: "there is a one-third probability that nobody will die, and a two-third probability that 600 people will die"

After reviewing the choices that were framed in this way, 78% of participants preferred program D, with the remaining 22% opting for program C.

The outcomes for Programs A and C are both identical, as are the outcomes for programs B and D. However, the change in how the decision frame was presented from positive to negative between the two groups produced a reversal in the preferences. When the programs were presented in terms of lives saved (think: positive frame), the participants preferred the perceived security of program A. When the programs were presented in terms of expected deaths (think: negative frame), participants chose the perceived gamble of program D.

In financial markets, corporations commonly rely on a positive framing effect when they announce a stock split. A stock split is a corporate action in which a company's existing shares are divided into multiple shares. Two-for-one is the most common form of a stock split. For example, a company with 500 shares currently trading at $10 per share will issue 500 additional shares, bringing the total to 1000 shares, which should result in the stock price trading at a revised $5 per share.

This price decline should occur because, although the number of shares outstanding has increased, the total dollar value capitalization of the shares and the underlying financial condition of the company remains the same as the pre-split value. There was no additional investment value added as a result of the split.

In a study (Garcia de Andoain 2009) that evaluated the effectiveness of corporate stock split announcements, it was shown that "after an announcement of an upcoming split, share prices increased, which was caused by investors that reacted favourably to the announcement by buying more shares".[25]

The announcement of a stock split frames the perception that investors have about the shares in a positive way, since they will now have *more* of the investment. Ironically, a stock split can result in increased trading costs for individual investors when they buy and sell the corporation's shares in the marketplace. This occurs because trading costs are frequently based solely on the number of shares traded, rather than the value.

Mental Accounting – "Saving For a Vacation"

Mental accounting refers to the process whereby individual investors separate their investment assets into segments by using subjective criteria, like the source of the money or the intent for how portions of it will be used.

Individuals often have a separate savings account set aside with money that will be used for such special occasions as a vacation, while still owing substantial debt that may be accruing high rates of interest. Money in the separate account is being treated differently from the money that could be used to reduce the debt. It does not make financial sense to have savings in an account, while at the same time be required to pay interest that is accruing on debt. Rather than saving for a vacation, the most rational decision would be to use the funds in the separate account to pay the debt and then borrow again at a future date to take the vacation. Most individuals understand the financial error they are making, yet they still have the separate accounts. Why?

The irrational decision is the result of a desire for self-discipline. It is an attempt by your logical brain to overcome the impulsive nature of the automatic brain, even if this need for self-control results in a poor financial decision.

Some individual investors will also divide their investments between a conservative investment portfolio and a speculative portfolio, in an attempt to somehow segregate investment losses (think: loss aversion). Despite all this effort, the investor's total wealth will be no different than if all the investments were held in a combined portfolio. Money is interchangeable and investment returns are cumulative, regardless of the account of origin.

Ambiguity Aversion – "I Prefer the Devil I Know"

Benjamin Franklin is given credit for stating "the only things certain in life are death and taxes". Without a doubt, the amount of uncertainty in our world has increased substantially since those words were first spoken, but what actually is uncertainty?

Uncertainty can be categorized in two ways:

- Aleatory uncertainty - where an outcome is associated with luck or chance.

- Epistemic uncertainty - where outcome is associated with a lack of knowledge.

The uncertainty associated with the outcome of a coin toss is an example of aleatory uncertainty, whereas not knowing the exact temperature in another city is an example of epistemic uncertainty.

The economist Frank Knight was the first to make a distinction between the decisions individuals make under conditions of *risk* rather than under definitions of *uncertainty*.[26]

Knight defined risk as an environment where the mathematical probabilities of all possible outcomes are known, while uncertainty is an environment where the likelihood of different outcomes cannot be expressed with any mathematical precision.

Without a doubt, epistemic uncertainty can be reduced in some situations through research and by acquiring knowledge. However, in many decision making environments, this is simply not possible.

A study by Daniel Ellsberg (1961), found that individuals clearly distinguish between risky options and uncertain options and have a clear preference for more certainty when making decisions. He called this behaviour "ambiguity aversion".[27]

Ambiguity aversion differs from risk aversion. This bias reflects our rejection of types of risk because of the absence of a measure of certainty, not because of the absolute size of the risk. Individuals have a preference to accept known risks over unknown risks.

Ellsberg constructed an experiment with an urn that contained balls of three different colours. The urn contained thirty red balls and sixty other balls that were either black or yellow. Participants in the experiment did not know how many black or yellow balls there were in the urn, but they were told that the total number of black balls plus the total number of yellow equalled sixty. The balls were mixed so that each was as likely to be drawn at random as any other. The subjects were told that they would have the opportunity to make two draws from the urn.

For the first draw, they were then given a choice between these two gambles:

> *Gamble A:* Receive $100 for drawing a red ball

> *Gamble B:* Receive $100 for drawing a black ball

For the second draw, they were then given a choice between these two gambles:

> *Gamble C:* Receive $100 for drawing a red or yellow ball

> *Gamble D:* Receive $100 for drawing a black or yellow ball

The experiment presents a participant with a situation of uncertainty:

- Are the balls that are not red either all yellow or all black? There is no mathematical formula available to calculate the probability.

The experiment also presents a participant with a situation of risk:

- Is a ball red or not red? This has a probability of occurrence of one-third vs. two-thirds.

If the participants were rational in the approach to making the selection between the choices, they would assume a projected probability that:

- The balls that were not red are equally likely to be yellow or black.

- And then calculate an expected monetary dollar value of the two gambles.

Since the monetary reward was exactly the same, it should follow that the participants should prefer Gamble A to Gamble B, if they believed that drawing a red ball is more likely than drawing a black ball.

Similarly it follows that participants should prefer Gamble C to Gamble D, if they believed that drawing a red or yellow ball is more likely than drawing a black or yellow ball.

It rationally follows that if you select Gamble A over Gamble B, then you should also select Gamble C over Gamble D. Conversely, if you would select Gamble D over Gamble C, then you should select Gamble B to Gamble A.

All the gambles involve risk. Whichever gamble is selected, the monetary reward for winning is the same ($100) and the cost of losing it is also the same ($0). Therefore, there are only two possible outcomes: either the participants receive some amount of money; or they receive nothing.

This experiment came to be known as the Ellsberg Paradox, since the results showed that most participants prefer Gamble A to Gamble B, and Gamble D to Gamble C.

Since the exact chances of winning are known for Gambles A and D, and not known for Gambles B and C, Ellsberg concluded that this was evidence an aversion to ambiguity was present in most individuals. He also demonstrated that this phenomenon only occurred when the choices that are available allow for the comparison of an ambiguous alternative to a less vague alternative.

In the absence of any information about probabilities, all possible outcomes can be assumed to be equally likely to occur. Situations that allow for the occurrence of a broad range of possible outcomes are vague and uncomfortable environments for you to make decisions. Therefore, in your world you try and change these situations from *uncertain* to merely *risky* by complacently accepting the fallacy that you can somehow overcome ambiguity by applying mathematical models, or calculate odds for all circumstances. The all too frequent result of this process is you being surprised by an unexpected future outcome and asking, "How could that have been possible?"

CHAPTER 3

MATHEMATICS + UNCERTAINTY ≠ RISK

"Life is a school of probability."

Walter Bagehot, entrepreneur and author

What Is Randomness?

Your world can be a confusing place. Randomness creates a form of uncertainty and is everywhere, yet it is hard for you to know whether an event is truly a random occurrence. Many outcomes that you experience are as much a result of random factors as they are from your decision making skill and proper analysis. The reality you perceive is not always caused by a direct connection between your actions and the desired outcome. As a result, the past is not always easy to understand and the future is actually much harder to predict than you realize.

There is a difference between a process that is random and one which *appears* to be random. Apple learned this lesson with the original shuffling method that it programmed into its iPods. True random sequences can produce repetition, but when iPod listeners heard the same song by an artist repeated back to back, they did not believe that the process was random. The solution was for the company to make the feature "less random to feel more random" according to Apple founder Steve Jobs.[28]

The fact that human decision making is not well suited to situations involving uncertainty was known as early as the 1930s. Individuals do not have accurate perceptions of what random sequences look like and cannot make up a sequence of numbers that pass mathematical tests for randomness.[29]

How can your brain cope with randomness? One way would be to simply accept uncertainty and base all of your beliefs in modesty. This would require you to accept that you actually know very little and that your understanding of the cause of events can be flawed. However, as humans we like to believe that we have control over our own destiny and environments, even when that belief requires us to delude ourselves.

Consequently, you cope by trying to derive more assurance of a known outcome, even from random processes. Your brain tends to look for and create a definite cause for every stimulus it receives. Your logical brain has a difficult time accepting that the outcome you perceive may be from unrelated or completely random factors.

In order to convince your logical brain that you are overcoming randomness, you collect as much information as you can before making a decision, since your logical brain believes that more data will always lead to more accurate decision choices. If you view your world under the framework of Knight's definitions of *uncertainty* and *risk* (think: *risk* is defined with mathematical probabilities, while *uncertainty* cannot be defined mathematically), you will then combine the collected data with the reliable predictability of numbers, in an attempt to change your environment from one which is *uncertain*, to one which is merely *risky*. The concepts of chance and probability are closely connected to randomness.

Think of how investment strategists and financial advisors refer to markets: they are *risky*, not *uncertain*. A financial advisor will try to evaluate your *risk* tolerance, not your *uncertainty* tolerance. The term *risk* conveys a feeling of control to your logical brain about the potential outcomes of your decisions, because mathematical odds allow you to determine the probable outcomes of events and to then make choices based upon these mathematical facts.

While uncertainty can be reduced in some situations, can everything that is currently present in your world and all possible events that may occur in the future be known today through a mathematical formula?

The realistic answer to this question is that there are limits to the accuracy of predicting events far into the future, due to the complexity of our modern world. The unpredictable and sometimes random ways events unfold do not always allow them to be subject to mathematical and probability calculations.

The Illusion of Control

The illusion of control is the tendency for individuals to overestimate their ability to control events. As a result, they feel that they can control outcomes over which they actually have no influence (think: over confidence). This effect was named by psychologist Ellen Langer who observed it in several studies she completed.

In an experiment by Langer and Roth (1975), participants were asked to predict the outcome of thirty coin tosses. The participants in the study were Yale University students, so we would presume that they are intelligent, well-educated individuals who should have an understanding of the basic law of probability that affects coin toss outcomes.[30]

The participants were unaware that the process was rigged so that each subject was right exactly half the time. However, different groups of participants were told that their success occurred at different places in the sequence. One group was told that their early guesses were accurate, while another group was told that their successes were distributed evenly through the thirty trials. After the thirty coin tosses were completed, both groups were surveyed about their performance. Subjects in the group that experienced early *success* in guessing the outcome of the tosses overestimated their total success and had higher expectations of how they would perform on future guessing games. In fact, 40% of all the participants in this experiment believed their performance on this chance task would improve with practice and 25% said that distractions would impair their performance.

Langer explained the findings in terms of the confusion between skill and chance that occurs in circumstances that require individuals to make decisions in the face of uncertainty. Since there is a fundamental clash between your need to feel in control and your ability to recognize randomness, you can easily be deceived to mistake skill for luck.

When you are in the grasp of the illusion of control, instead of searching for ideas to prove yourself wrong, you usually attempt to prove yourself correct (think: confirmation bias). The ambiguous evidence of the success was used by participants in Langer's experiment to support their idea that they had some ability to correctly forecast random coin tosses.

Is this a much different situation than when you congratulate yourself for your superior investing abilities after watching a stock you just purchased begin to appreciate in price?

Do You Really Understand Probability?

You would think that as you get older and wiser your life experiences would allow you to obtain a more accurate understanding of probability. Unfortunately, this is rarely the result. Perhaps it's your automatic brain at work again, getting in the way before your logical brain can calculate a solution? Or maybe your automatic brain is not allowing you to absorb the details necessary to gain this knowledge?

Your automatic brain tends to focus on the excitement of changes in the size of a potential reward, but is much less sensitive to changes in the probability of receiving the reward. Accordingly, your center of attention is on how big the reward is, rather than how likely it is that you will actually receive it. This is the reason why lotteries can advertise for ticket buyers by simply broadcasting the size of the jackpot and not much else.[31]

Your mind's eye will create an image of what would happen if you won the jackpot (think: availability bias). The more information you receive that makes the mental picture more vivid, results in the event seeming more probable, even though the details of the information you have obtained do not actually support the outcome. Just because you can intensely imagine winning a jackpot, does not increase the probability that it will actually occur. In an attempt to ground yourself once again by some form of self-discipline, your logical brain eventually becomes active and tries to calculate the probability that you will actually be buying the Ferrari that your automatic brain is dreaming about.

The Lotto Max lottery has a minimum jackpot of $10 million, but frequently has a jackpot prize of over $50 million. Ticket buyers get to choose seven numbers between 1 and 49. The odds of choosing the winning seven numbers and having the sole winning ticket in a draw are about 1 in 28,633,528.

I'll let your automatic brain and your logical brain wrestle over those numbers, but it's likely that you will still buy the occasional ticket. Your automatic brain will eventually trump your logical brain's understanding of the remote odds by convincing yourself that "you can't win without a ticket" or "someone has to win, it might as well be me"

Presentation Matters

Your brain will respond differently depending on how numerical sequences are presented to you.

We can struggle to understand odds when they are presented as percentages or as frequencies (1 in 2). Researchers have conducted experiments to determine which type of numerical presentation will elicit the greatest confidence in individuals and which would lead to the most accurate conclusions. They found that as we had to work harder to process data presented in a frequency format, this lead to higher confidence in our judgments.[32]

At first glance, percentages appear easier for you to understand. However, percentages tend to be more abstract and are subsequently more difficult to use to create a mental picture in your mind's eye. As a result, you tend to average the percentage data, since it is relatively easy to do so, but this is not always the best choice to reach an accurate conclusion.

When data is presented as a frequency, most individuals are unable to calculate an average, since the mental calculation is more difficult and requires multiple mathematical steps. However, it is easier to visualize frequency data in your mind's eye compared to percentage data, so the extra mathematical effort that is required is rewarded by producing a more accurate answer. As a result, this information can then be used to make a more accurate decision choice.

This difference in how your brain will respond to sequence data presentation formats has practical implications. For example, if the goal of the presentation is to highlight a *risk*, it is best to use the frequency format, since your brain will make a calculation that is relatively more accurate.

Framing can also influence how you view data presentations. If you are told that "35 times out of 100 an investment strategy fails" this tends to have a more negative frame than being told "65% of the time this strategy is successful". Therefore, if you are told that "35 times out of 100 an investment strategy fails" your decision choice is likely to be affected by both your more accurate understanding of the odds calculation of the data, but also by the negative frame in which it was presented.

The next time a financial advisor presents a data sequence to you as an evidence for accepting a *risky* choice, try reversing the format of the presentation and the frame that is being used, so that you truly have an accurate understanding of the choice.

Now You See It, Now You Don't

Patterns of all kinds are present throughout your world. Mathematics is often referred to as the science of patterns, since patterns are frequently required as a unifying theme in many mathematical concepts.

A number pattern, such as 5, 10, 15, 20, 25, will seem very familiar to you, because it is a pattern type that you learn early in your life. As your mathematical learning increases, you encounter broader and more complicated patterns.

Your understanding begins with logic patterns. As a child, you can distinguish between which objects are triangles and which are squares, before you can learn to count each type.

A logic pattern can be based on the characteristics of various objects (think: shape) or on order (think: sequences). Mathematics is a useful prediction tool and number patterns are all about prediction. If you see the sequence 5, 10, 15, 20, 25, what will the 6th number of this pattern be? Your likely guess will be "30".

If you can identify a pattern when you look at a number sequence, you would then use this pattern to generalize what you have detected to create a broader solution to a problem.

Look at the following sequence of numbers:

1   1   2   3   5   8   13   21   34

Do you detect a pattern?

This sequence is called Fibonacci numbers and was named after Leonardo of Pisa (also known as Fibonacci), who introduced the sequence in 1202.

The first two Fibonacci numbers are 0 and 1, and each subsequent number is the sum of the previous two.

1   1   2   3   5   8   13   21   34

1+1=2   1+2=3   3+2=5   5+3=8   8+5=13   13+8=21   21+13=34   Etc.

The Fibonacci sequence occurs frequently in nature and the underlying principle is sometimes used in financial markets trading algorithms. It is a useful mathematical pattern that has practical applications.

Look at the following sequence of numbers:

11148251115423111097811145761112 4671119873

Do you detect a pattern? How about now?

1114825**111**5423**111**0978**111**4576**111**2467**111**9873

The pattern shows a series of three consecutive "111"s that appear after each grouping of four other numbers. What do the "111" clusters signify and how are they used to determine the next four numbers in the sequence?

This sequence is called a Fustey sequence and I typed random numbers after each "111" cluster. It should be easy to detect this pattern, but the pattern has no significance other than to illustrate how simple it can be to detect a numerical pattern.

When you view the outcome of a random process, be it coin flips, number sequences or charts of stock prices, you may detect *patterns* that you believe have meaning. These patterns are both highly convincing and highly subjective. Any mathematical formula you use to convert the pattern from a state of uncertainty to a state that is merely risky is an illusion. Nothing like this has really occurred. You have simply deluded yourself into having a feeling of control that will result in a poor decision choice.

Missed It, By That Much

Although mathematical measurement can be very precise, there is always some degree of uncertainty in any measurement process, which is rarely focused upon when the results are presented. For example, most investors have seen a breaking news headline such as this:

"U.S. non-farm payroll employment increased in August by 58,000 workers and the unemployment rate declined 0.1 to 9.6 percent."

But you will likely never see an additional comment which follows the headline that states:

"Such a small change is not statistically significant, so the U.S. Bureau of Labor Statistics cannot tell whether 58,000 jobs were actually created or the headline number is simply the result of a measurement error."

The U.S. Bureau of Labor Statistics (BLS) Employment Statistics program is designed to measure trends in employment. Each month the BLS surveys approximately 150,000 businesses and government agencies (the establishment survey) and also surveys 60,000 households (the household survey).[33]

The BLS begins collecting survey reports for a reference month as soon as the previous reference period is complete. Collection times range from 9 to 15 days, depending on the scheduled date for the next news release. Given this short collection cycle for the first preliminary estimates, many businesses are not able to provide their payroll information in time to be included in the initial estimates. Therefore, survey responses for the reference month continue to be collected for two more months, and are then incorporated into a second preliminary and then a final estimate, which are published in subsequent months. These additional responses are the primary sources of the monthly revisions.

The establishment survey and household survey both produce sample-based estimates of employment. A monthly employment change of about 100,000 is considered statistically significant in the establishment survey, while the threshold for a statistically significant change in the household survey is about 400,000.

If the actual number of new jobs that are created in any reference month is less than the statistically significant thresholds, then this might have been caused by a pure statistical accident. The level of statistical significance is determined by the probability that any change that occurred was not the result of some type of simple sampling error. Therefore, any time the employment rate statistic changes by a one-tenth of a percentage, the only way to tell whether a change that small was actually worth paying attention to or is possibly just a measurement error, is to understand the statistical significance of the methodology by which the data was collected.

Now contemplate again about CNBC's clock countdown to the release of the employment report (think: availability bias). Will making an investment decision based on the release of this statistic improve the profitability of your investment decision? Will it help change your investment decision making environment from uncertain to merely risky?

Let's Toss a Coin

A coin has two sides. We refer to them as "heads" or "tails" and we frequently use the process of tossing a coin as a fair way to decide outcomes when we want an unbiased decision. But do we really understand the law of probability that determines the outcome of even a simple coin toss?

There are only two possible outcomes of a toss (either heads or tails), so the probability of getting heads on a single toss is exactly $\frac{1}{2}$ (one in two). It follows then, that the probability of getting two heads in two tosses is $\frac{1}{4}$ (one in four) and the probability of getting three heads in three tosses is $\frac{1}{8}$ (one in eight). If we toss the coin one more time and heads appears again, it is a probability of $\frac{1}{16}$ (one in sixteen).

We have now tossed a coin four times and each time it has come up heads. If the next toss is a head that would be five in a row, which has a probability of $\frac{1}{32}$ (one in thirty-two). So must a tail be due?

The odds of a fifth consecutive head now have to be much less than when we started our flipping game, so seeing a tail on the next flip must be greater than the $\frac{1}{2}$ (one in two) chance that was present when the game began. Is this a correct assumption?

The odds are still ½ (one in two). Any reasoning that it is more likely that the next toss will be a tail than a head is based on knowing the outcomes of the previous tosses. You know what the previous tosses were, but the coin does not. These past outcomes do not have any influence on the odds in the future. Individuals have a mental image that coin flips should always be roughly equal, so they tend to believe that the fifth toss will more likely be a tail because a tail is *due* (think: representativeness bias).

Although the odds of a sequence of five consecutive tosses being all heads is only $\frac{1}{32}$, it is only that probability before the coin is first tossed. After the first four tosses the results are no longer unknown, so the probability of either a head or a tail occurring in any future toss is unchanged at ½.

When individuals are asked to create a random looking sequence of coin tosses, they tend to make a sequence where the proportion of heads to tails stays close to 50% in any short segment. If the sequence was instead predicted solely by chance, the relatively even occurrence would not be present. Many individuals falsely believe that short sequences of random events should be representative of longer ones.[34]

The Law of Large Numbers

In Jakob Bernoulli's 1713 work Ars Conjectandi (The Art of Conjecture) he described a probability theory called the "Golden Theorem". This theorem eventually became known as *the law of large numbers,* since it was based on the way results reflect underlying probabilities when a large number of trials are performed. As the number of trials of a random process increases, the percentage difference between the expected and actual values goes to zero.

For example, the law of large numbers suggests that as a company's revenue grows, its chances of sustaining a large percentage rate of growth will diminish. This is based on the simple premise that as a company's revenues continue to increase, it must expand exponentially just to maintain a constant percentage of growth. Therefore, as revenue grows the chance of sustaining the current rates of growth in the future diminishes.

Unbounded corporate earnings growth is not realistic. Although growth may initially be exponential, at some point, either an unforeseen negative change in demand for a product, or production limits that are required to meet demand, will decrease the rate of growth.

Based On 35% Projected Growth, We Have Increased Our Target Price

All investments have only one purpose, which is to produce cash flows. These cash flows may be fixed (think: bond interest rates) or variable (think: stock dividends).

The prices for which stock investments trade on financial markets are set by investors based on their estimates of the expected future value of the cash flows. Financial market analysts also publish earnings estimates, which are frequently used by investors as their basis for determining the future cash flows that will be available.

An earnings estimate is an analyst's expectation of what a company will earn on a quarterly or annual basis. This estimate is calculated by looking at previous earnings statements, market conditions for the industry in which the company operates, and developments that are specific to the company, in order to estimate the future net income of the company over a future period of time.

A basic earnings per share (EPS) calculation for a company is:

EPS = Net Earnings / Outstanding Shares

If a company has earnings of $100 and 10 shares outstanding, then the EPS is $10 ($100 / 10 = 10). An analyst will then use the EPS to calculate a price earnings (P/E) ratio to determine a basic valuation for the shares:

P/E = Market Price per share/EPS

If a company is currently trading at $90 a share and has earnings per share (EPS) of $10, the P/E ratio for the stock would be 9 ($90/$10).

Financial market participants are usually more concerned with what will happen in the future to a company's share price, than what has happened previously, so analysts will next calculate a forward P/E ratio based on their projection of future earnings.

Forward P/E = Market Price per share/ Projected future EPS

If a company is currently trading at $90 a share and has projected future earnings per share (EPS) of $15, the forward P/E ratio for the stock would be 6 ($90/$15).

The forward P/E is sometimes referred to as a "multiple", because it shows how much investors are willing to pay per share for each dollar of earnings. Generally, a high P/E suggests that investors are expecting higher earnings growth in the future, compared to companies with a lower P/E.

Financial advisors use the forward EPS, forward P/E, and the resulting projected future share price target that are contained in analyst research reports as the basis for recommending commission-generating purchase or sale transactions in your investment portfolio. Frequently you will read these types of comments in the reports:

"The company has $57 million in cash and only 100 million in long-term debt. However its valuation is not cheap, trading at 35 times projected 2011 earnings. Normally, we would consider a multiple that high as a rich valuation, but when we take into account the 5-year projected annual revenue growth rate is 39%, 35 times earnings starts to appear to be a bargain."

The fly in the ointment with the research report process is that analysts are also individuals who are subject to the same representativeness, availability, over-confidence and herding biases as you and I. Therefore, in many circumstances the estimated future growth rates that analysts are using are based on unrealistic exponentially expanding rates of growth for many years into the future. In fact, the growth rates that analysts use for their projections are not grounded by the reality of the law of large numbers. Since these projections are for periods that often extend into the future for periods up to five years, even a small error in the projected growth rate will have significant negative consequences for the future earnings and share price target. Studies (Shane et al 2009) have demonstrated that long-term forecasts of analysts are optimistically biased, grossly inaccurate and generally meaningless.[35]

As a result, individual investors who use these estimates and projections as the basis for their investment decisions are likely to be disappointed in the outcome of their investments.

Gambler's Fallacy

Representativeness bias is also associated with the law of large numbers through the concept of *Gambler's Fallacy*. The fallacy results from a misinterpretation of the law of large numbers, by which individuals believe that the theory applies to both large and small samples, when it does not.

If the probability of throwing a double-6 with two dice is 1/36, then the more times you throw the dice, the closer in proportion will be the number of double-6s thrown to that of the total number of throws. Ignoring the words *in proportion* in the above definition leads to much misunderstanding among individual investors and gamblers.

Gambler's Fallacy lies in the idea that over long periods of time chances will somehow even out. If you toss your coin 100 times and you see 60 heads and 40 tails, most individuals believe that more tails are now due for the sequence to get equal. The belief is that the *law* of averages really is a law, which ensures that over long periods the totals of both heads and tails will eventually become even.

This is not how it works. In fact, the opposite is true. As the number of tosses gets larger, the probability is that the percentage of heads or tails thrown will approach 50%, but the difference between the actual number of heads or tails thrown and the number that represents 50% will get larger. How can that be?

More Coin Tosses

Imagine that you continue tossing the coin from the previous example (60 heads and 40 tails) and the next 100 results are 56 heads and 44 tails. The percentage of heads has decreased from 60% to 58%. However, there are now 32 more heads than tails, while there were only 20 more in the first 100 tosses. The number of tails less than heads has now increased by 12, but the percentage of heads to tails has decreased.

If the next hundred tosses results in 50 heads and 50 tails, the equalization is still missing, since there will be 166 heads in 300 tosses or 55%, but the number of times tails has appeared is still 32 less than heads. The law of averages does not ensure a concept of *fairness,* so that the number of tails will eventually increase to equal the number of heads. The process is not self-correcting. Deviations that have occurred over shorter time frames are merely diluted over a longer time horizon.

You would likely not be overly surprised by the result of 60% heads after 100 tosses, but you would be if after a million tosses there were still 60% heads. You would expect the deviation from 50% to be smaller. Similarly, after 100 tosses, you would not be surprised if the difference between heads and tails is 20. However, after a million tosses you would likely have an expectation that the difference would be much larger than 20.

The key to understanding these coin tossing results is the independence of each toss. A chance event is not influenced by the events which have occurred previously. If a die has not shown a "5" for 30 throws, the probability of a 5 appearing is still 1/6 on the 31st throw.

After watching a stock rise for an extended period, have you ever said to yourself, or seen a media quote of a professional investment manager who says, "I'll buy that stock when it declines. I'm sure a correction is due."

Don't expect the law of large numbers to make it happen.

Size Does Matter

Extraordinary events do not always require extraordinary causes. Given enough time, they can happen by chance.

If sample size is large enough, it is possible (both in theory and in reality) to have the most unimaginable event occur.

The odds of looking at your cards in a poker game and seeing that you have been dealt a straight flush are 1 in 649,739. The odds are extreme, but they can be calculated precisely. Yet, if you think about the number of poker hands that have been played since the game was invented, is there any doubt that a straight flush has been dealt? Is there any doubt that a straight flush is even dealt every day, given the number of poker games that are played around the world in person and on the internet? In games of chance and in financial market investing, it is the absolute size of a sample that matters.

Most individuals interpret *rare* to mean something that is not likely. When you make decisions, you interpret the chances of encountering rare events in dramatically different ways.

If you learn about the likelihood of encountering a low-probability, high-impact event from descriptions that include precise probabilities, then the information you receive tends to fit a mental image you create of the event. If you receive more details, it makes the event seem more probable, even though the information you have obtained may not directly support the outcome. As a result, you tend to overestimate (by a lot) the chances of that event actually occurring.

However, in most circumstances, when you need to choose between uncertain outcomes, you do not usually make your decision based only on precise mathematical probabilities. Instead, you make decisions based on your own previous experiences. Unfortunately, these experiences can distort your perception and result in a decision that is dramatically different from one that is only the consequence of using probabilities. You will overestimate the chances of hitting the jackpot, but you will also underestimate the chance of experiencing a large investment loss when you are given the same probabilities.[36]

This tendency is reinforced in circumstances where you are repeatedly exposed to feedback from small decisions. If you only receive a small sample of possible results, then you slowly update your mental images to reflect only the results you have experienced. The relative rarity of an event lulls you into underestimating the dangers of it occurring.

Think of how casino slot machines operate. These machines pay out small amounts of money regularly, to provide positive feedback to gamblers on a frequent basis. The small payouts reinforce the gambler's mental image that a jackpot cannot be far from occurring. This is why a gambler often tries to save his machine by tilting his chair against it when he leaves for a short time. "Don't play *my* machine, its due!"

Now imagine a slot machine that only paid out one huge jackpot on a rare occasion. There would not be any small, but frequent, positive feedback received by a gambler. As a result, most would decide that the machine was not very likely to pay a jackpot anytime soon and give up.

Our life experiences exert a surprisingly powerful and under-appreciated influence on how we decide between uncertain outcomes, so we adopt different decision making strategies to deal with life's shifting uncertainties. The result is that we unknowingly misapply the lessons of life.

Stock markets are environments in which most individual investors tend to learn by experience (think: the gambling experiment). Extreme events, like the single day 22% decline of the Dow Jones Industrial Average that occurred on October 19th, 1987, are not experienced very often, so the opportunity to learn from them is relatively rare. Your expectation of the relative probability of these really bad things happening in financial markets is generally much lower than both the actual probabilities, and the discouraging historical evidence that they actually do occur more frequently than you or the your financial advisor would expect.

Now think again about the concept of being dealt a straight flush in poker and reframe these odds so that they now represent a poor investment outcome. With the vast number of shares trading in world financial markets each and every day, is there any doubt that unexpected and unimaginably poor results are occurring for some investor?

If you have never experienced a memorably poor result from your investment decisions, then you should consider yourself just lucky, not wise.

Frequency Matters Too

"The most powerful force in the universe is compound interest"

Albert Einstein, scientist

I'll accept Albert Einstein's belief regarding the importance of compounding, but do you actually understand the concept, especially when it is shown in a numerical sequence?

The concept of a compounding investment is a repetitive process by which new earnings are continually added to the total investment, so as to form a larger base on which future earnings accumulate. The result is that as earnings are reinvested, they then produce their own earnings.

Examples of different compounding growth rates are often shown to you in tables similar to the one below. The table shows the results of annual compounding rates of return for an initial investment of $1,000.

Year	5%	10%	15%	20%	25%	30%
0	$1,000	$1,000	$1,000	$1,000	$1,000	$1,000
1	$1,050	$1,100	$1,150	$1,200	$1,250	$1,300
2	$1,103	$1,210	$1,323	$1,440	$1,563	$1,690
3	$1,158	$1,331	$1,521	$1,728	$1,953	$2,197
4	$1,216	$1,464	$1,749	$2,074	$2,441	$2,856
5	$1,276	$1,611	$2,011	$2,488	$3,052	$3,713
6	$1,340	$1,772	$2,313	$2,986	$3,815	$4,827
7	$1,407	$1,949	$2,660	$3,583	$4,768	$6,275
8	$1,477	$2,144	$3,059	$4,300	$5,960	$8,157
9	$1,551	$2,358	$3,518	$5,160	$7,451	$10,604
10	$1,629	$2,594	$4,046	$6,192	$9,313	$13,768
15	$2,079	$4,177	$8,137	$15,407	$28,422	$51,186
20	$2,653	$6,727	$16,367	$38,338	$86,736	$190,050
25	$3,386	$10,835	$32,919	$95,396	$264,698	$705,641
30	$4,322	$17,449	$66,212	$237,376	$807,794	$2,619,996
35	$5,516	$28,102	$133,176	$590,668	$2,465,190	$9,727,860
40	$7,040	$45,259	$267,864	$1,469,772	$7,523,164	$36,118,865

The Table illustrates why Albert Einstein made his comment. The results of achieving an additional 5% annual growth over an entire investment time horizon are remarkable, particularly at the higher rates. The result of capital growth of 15% plus an additional 5% in compound earnings would be identical to the return produced from 20% in capital growth alone.

This provides a compelling argument for the reinvestment of any distributed earnings (interest, dividends and capital gains) from an investment. For this reason, the fine print of historical investment returns that are presented to you by a financial advisor will frequently assume compounding growth rates, regardless of whether this is likely to occur in your personal circumstances or not.

Is It That Simple?

Interest rates are complex. Our assumption is that compounding is always occurring at a consistent, positive rate of return and will always occur at exactly the same frequency over a very long-term time horizon to get the desired results. Is this how investments really work?

The first column in the compounding table assumed that you had $1000 and were paid 5% per year. That means that you received $50 in the first year, but is it really $50?

Or is it $4.167 each month, or $25 for January to June and $25 for July to December? But if it was $25 at the end of June, then you would have had $1025 in July and yet only earn another $25 during the rest of the year. So do $1000 and $1025 then earn the same amount in 6 months? That can't be possible, can it?

Annual-Percentage-A-What?

There are two basic terms that you need to understand when discussing interest rates and compounding:

- The annual percentage rate (APR). This is the rate of return that is quoted to you.

- The annual percentage yield (APY). This is the rate of return you receive after all compounding is taken into account for a year, or the total return that you will receive.

The APY will always be greater than or equal to the APR.

Your friendly neighbourhood bank always uses the concepts of APR and APY when they discuss loans. The APR is the rate that the bank quotes to you, while the APY is what you actually pay. Read the fine print in the agreement carefully the next time you apply for a credit card. And, of course, banks will always advertise the rate that looks more appealing to you.

However, when you invest in a term deposit, the rate quoted will be the APY, because it will appear to be a higher rate. Have you ever seen a bank advertisement for an accelerated rate or step-up term deposit? These types of investments quote an annual interest rate (APR) that increases each year of the term. The interest rate in the first year is usually very low, but the interest rate in the final year is high - often triple the rate payable in year one.

What counts is the APY because the low interest rate paid in the initial years of the investment results in the actual return that you receive being lower than the high APR rate that is paid in the final years.

Do you think that this may be trying to appeal to your mental shortcuts (think: framing)? The APY is what matters to you and this is what you should use to compare investments.

Simple, Compound and Velocity

Simple interest pays a fixed amount over time. For example:

A bond with a face value of $1000 and a 5% interest rate pays you $50 each year until it matures.

Simple interest is the most basic type of return.

You begin with an investment of $1000 and earn $50 each year. However, the $50 each year does not participate to enhance your future investment. Only the original $1000 produces the return over the term of the bond and, as a result, there is no compounding.

With simple interest there is no difference between APR and APY distinction, since your investment earnings do not change. You always earn the same amount every year.

Now frame the rate of interest your investment produces as the velocity of your return. It is a similar concept to speed when you are driving your car.

If you are driving at a speed of 100 km an hour, then you will travel 100 km each hour. If you are receiving 5% interest then you will earn 5% of your principal each year.

An interest rate provides an investment with a *speed* that it will follow. If you have $1000 at a 5% simple interest rate, your speed is $50/year. But you don't need to follow that pace for a full year. If your investment grew for only 6 months, you should be entitled to $25.

If you make a $1000 investment, then each year this investment receives $50. Your investment is moving at a speed of $50 each year. You can picture your return in your mind's eye as looking like a staircase, because you are only paid at the end of the year. Simple interest will always maintain the same speed of return.

I Want To Go Faster

Simple interest is rare in the investment world, since most investments allow you the opportunity to invest some or all your earnings once they are received. Many companies and mutual funds offer dividend reinvestment plans or you could use the interest received from a bond payment to make an additional investment.

The most basic type of compounding is a period-over-period return, or year-over-year. You would earn $50 at the end of the first year, which is the same as simple interest. However, by the end of the second year, your investment value is now $1,102.50, because both the original principal and the interest you received at the end of the first year were combined to produce a return for the next year. In following years, the rate of speed gradually increases. This deceptively small but cumulative growth makes compound interest extremely powerful. For this reason, losses of your initial capital, or periods of time where your investments do not earn a positive return, can have a very harmful effect on the likelihood of you achieving your long-term investment objectives.

The Rule of 72

As you have seen throughout this book, you use mental shortcuts to allow yourself to process the information you receive.

The Rule of 72 is widely used as a mathematical shortcut to help you with basic compound interest calculations. It is generally used to calculate how long it will take you to double your principal for a stated rate of return.

For example, if your investment is producing a 5% rate of return that compounds annually, then by using the rule of 72, you will calculate that your money will double in 14.4 years (Years to double = 72 / Interest Rate).

The rule can also be used to calculate a rate of return that is required to double your principal for a specified time frame. For example, to double your money in 10 years, you must receive an interest rate of 7.2% (10 years to double=72/10).

The rule can also be used to estimate the effects of inflation on the purchasing power of an investment. For example, if you retire and the rate of inflation is actually 3% rather than your projection of 2%, then your money will lose half its purchasing power in 24 years rather than the 36 years you expected (72/3= 24 vs. 72/2=36).

Rules Are Meant To Be Broken

The rule of 72 works well for many common interest rate estimations, because the numerical value of 72 is a convenient numerator. It can be easily divided by small numbers (1, 2, 3, 4, 6, 8, 9 and 12). The rule provides a good approximation for annual compounding at rates of return between 6% and 10%, but these approximations are less accurate at both lower and higher interest rates.

The Rule of 72 is actually a shortcut for the Rule of 70, while the Rule of 70 is actually a shortcut for the Rule of 69. The Rule of 69 is derived from the natural logarithm of 2, which is 0.693147. When dealing in percentages, this number becomes 69.3147.

You will not find many references to the more accurate Rule of 69.3 or even the short cut Rule of 69, because when it comes to mathematical shortcuts you want them to be as easy as possible.

Therefore the Rule of 72 is used instead of the Rule of 70, 69 or 69.3, as 72 has more whole numbers that it can be divided by (72, 36, 24, 18, 12, 9, 8 and 1) than 70 (70, 35, 14, 10, 7 and 1). The Rule of 72 is easier for individual investors to understand than the Rule of 70, even if the cost of simplicity is the accuracy of the results.

The Rules of the Rules of Thumb

Interest Rate	Actual Rate	Rule of 72	Rule of 70	Rule of 69.3
0.25%	277.605	288.000	280.000	277.200
0.5%	138.976	144.000	140.000	138.600
1%	69.661	72.000	70.000	69.300
2%	35.003	36.000	35.000	34.650
3%	23.450	24.000	23.333	23.100
4%	17.673	18.000	17.500	17.325
5%	14.207	14.400	14.000	13.860
6%	11.896	12.000	11.667	11.550
7%	10.245	10.286	10.000	9.900
8%	9.006	9.000	8.750	8.663
9%	8.043	8.000	7.778	7.700
10%	7.273	7.200	7.000	6.930
11%	6.642	6.545	6.364	6.300
12%	6.116	6.000	5.833	5.775
15%	4.959	4.800	4.667	4.620

- For low annual rates of return, the rule of 69.3 will be more accurate than 72.

- For an interest rate of 5%, you can use any of the rules.

- For interest rates between 6% and 10%, the Rule of 72 is reasonably accurate.

- The overall accuracy of the Rule of 72 declines as the rate of return increases.

- If a rate of return is negative, then the Rule of 70 is always more accurate than the Rule of 72.

- The Rule of 69 gives accurate results for any rate. This is because 69 is closer to 69.3%.

- For calculations where the rate of return is compounded daily rather than annually, the rules of 69, 69.3 or 70 are better than 72.

The Rule of 72 illustrates why mathematical shortcuts always have limitations. Even small differences in the calculations derived from these rules can result in systematic errors for individual investors when they are used to assist in making judgments about uncertain outcomes.

Correlation Is Not Causation. So Does Smoke Always Mean Fire?

Correlation is a statistical term that refers to the measurement of both the strength and the direction of a linear relationship between two variables. If two investments had a perfect correlation, their prices would be expected to increase and decrease in an equal fixed proportion over a certain period of time.

The phrase "*correlation does not imply causation*" is a reminder that just because a correlation between two variables can be measured, it does not always imply that one causes the other.

If you compare the shoe size of individuals and their mathematical ability, you will find a strong correlation. This occurs because they both initially increase with age until reaching a point where the correlation weakens.

Causality refers to whether one event actually causes another event to happen. Many individual investors and financial advisors frequently believe that *correlation proves causation* in financial markets, by their tendency to commonly believe that two events that occur together must have a causality or cause-and-effect relationship.

Representativeness bias plays a key role in why you are frequently misled by this logic fallacy. Let's look at an example:

- Event A: A financial strategist appears on CNBC and makes a prediction that the stock market will rise.

- Event B: Following the appearance by the strategist, the stock market rises.

In this example, a conclusion about causality (think: CNBC appearance = rising market) is made after observing only a correlation between the two events. Since Event A is observed to be correlated with Event B, it is assumed that A is causing B even though there is no evidence that actually supports the conclusion.

If Event A has not caused Event B, then what could have caused it?

There are at least four possibilities:

- Event B may be the cause of Event A.

- An unknown third factor (Event C) may actually be the cause of both Event A and Event B.

- Some combination of the above three relationships may be occurring. For example, Event B may be the cause of Event A, and simultaneously Event A is the cause of Event B. Why is it possible that the only relationship between Event A and Event B is that A causes B?

- Perhaps the entire linkage between Event A and Event B is nothing more than coincidence, where Event A and Event B are both occurring at the same time and there is no direct relationship to each other besides their simultaneous occurrence.

It is not always a simple process to determine causality in a real world environment, since there are often multiple causes for an event. Some of these causes may seem obvious at first glance, but others may never be observable. It's impossible to ever know with absolute certainty that all the causes that have determined an event have been correctly identified.

However, by isolating variables it is possible to reach a reasonable degree of certainty by which our confusing correlation and causation can be avoided.

Variables that identify causes are called *independent variables*, while effects are called *dependent variables*. Most environments, especially financial market environments, involve far more than just two variables. Therefore, an attempt should be made to try and control for effects using statistical analysis by isolating causes that are thought to be relevant. But if some variables are not presently known, or may not ever be observable, are we ever sure that all events are being considered?

Therefore, determining causation seems to require not just correlation between events, but also some other type of *counterfactual* dependence. What would have happened to the stock market if the financial strategist appeared at different times or on different days?

However, in many situations it is either not possible or not practical to make these types of changes, since the past cannot be altered. For this reason causation can only be incidental and never known with absolute certainty.

Digging For Fool's Gold

Data mining is the process of "digging" through data in order to discover previously unknown patterns. Over the past two decades, the rapid escalation of computer processing power has exponentially increased both data collection and storage capabilities. Digital databases now contain massive quantities of information.

Data mining has been used for many years by businesses (to identify consumer spending patterns to improve marketing) and by scientists (to detect causes and correlations with diseases).

Financial markets are rich sources for data mining, as major financial exchanges can produce millions of data points in very short time spans. In finance, data mining is often referred to as *optimization* and its goal is to identify correlations that can be used as filters for new trading rules. Data is clustered and screened by computer software looking to find new strategies that can then be used to identify future trading opportunities. However, the assumption of causality cannot be made on the basis of only correlated observations or a researcher's intuition.

Individual investors are repeatedly told of the discovery of new investment strategies that they should follow to make untold profits. However, when these strategies are found through data mining, there are a number of potential problems that can complicate the leap to successful implementation of the theory in future real world conditions:

- Was verification of the strategy corrupted by unknown interrelationships between variables in the data?

- Was the data sample used actually large enough? An unavoidable fact of data mining is that the data being analyzed may not be representative of a large sample and, therefore, it may not contain certain critical relationships that exist across larger sample sizes.

Frequently, a formula just happens to fit only the data of the past, and subsequently, this may not have any future predictive value. Patterns will occur in data by pure chance and, in many cases, data mining is immune to either statistical verification or rebuttal.[37]

Without *counterfactual* validation (being able to analyze the significance of a strategy that worked in the past without knowing how many other strategies were tested unsuccessfully), the true statistical significance can only be assessed after qualifying the number of undocumented previous failed attempts. If a researcher finds one rule that finally works after thousands of unsuccessful attempts with different strategies, is there really a *discovery?*

Back testing is a close cousin of data mining. It is the process of testing a new theorized trading strategy over previous time horizons, rather than looking for undiscovered information in past data. Instead of applying a strategy for a future time period, which could take years, a trader will perform a simulation of the trading strategy on past data in order to gauge its effectiveness.

Although the process of back testing appears valid, the reality is that if you go back far enough in time and create enough modifications to the original trading rule, a near perfect rule can always be created. Unfortunately, the outcome of this process is that the trading rule will likely not work reliably in the future, since there is no assurance that future market conditions will be exactly the same as the past. When you look backwards in time, you are usually only looking for confirmation of what you already believe to be true (think: confirmation bias).

Additional flaws in a trading rule that was produced from data mining can be detected by any of the following:[38]

- Any acknowledgement by the researchers that they tweaked their model to get better results, such as adding additional variables as the testing progressed to improve results.

- A valid strategy must have a plausible theory to explain why it worked previously and also why it will continue to be successful. For example, if it works with U.S. stocks last year, will it also work with Canadian stocks this year?

- Were the data mining results *layered*? Layering occurs by adding variables to previous data mining results to further increase the success rate of the previous findings.

- Will transaction costs offset the value of any trading rule that was discovered?

Of course, the most obvious flaw in the discovery of a new trading rule is, why would the discoverer tell other investors about it?

By mining enough data and alternative trading theories, successful trading rules can be found solely by chance.

In February 1978, a new investment strategy was unveiled that provided the methodology for a breakthrough in financial market forecasting. The strategy would allow any investor by the end of January to determine whether the Dow Jones Industrial Average would rise or fall by the end of that calendar year. There was historical proof of the strategy, since the methodology had correctly predicted the direction of the market in each of the past eleven years.[39]

This system seemed like a sure thing: it was simple to use and for eleven consecutive years after it was revealed, it proved accurate. It stumbled in 1990 when it was wrong, but redeemed itself by being accurate once again from 1991 to 1998. Since then, the record has been a little less successful, but overall in 33 of the past 41 years since it was unveiled, the system has had an accuracy rate of over 80%!

With such an incredible success rate, there must be a high rate of causality between the cause and effect of the system, so you should have enough confidence to invest your entire life savings by this trading rule. Or should you?

If you are an NFL football fan you might, since the cause and effect for this strategy was *discovered* by a sports writer named Leonard Koppett and is based on the winner of the Super Bowl that is played near the end of each January.

Prior to 1970, there existed two separate football leagues: the American Football League (AFL) and the National Football League (NFL). The winners of each league met in the Super Bowl. Once the AFL merged into the NFL in 1970 to create a single league, Koppett's Super Bowl indicator theory stated that if a team from the old NFL wins the Super Bowl, the stock market will rise. Conversely, if a team with roots to the AFL wins, the stock market will fall the rest of the year.

At the same time, Koppett also unveiled a similar stock market prediction methodology that was based on an increase or decrease in major league batting averages, but this theory faded quickly from view as the success rate was much less.

Koppett's article was really an attempt at humour and to show why statistics in sports have little real value. Despite this fact, you can be assured that the financial media will discuss the results of the Super Bowl predictor the day after the results of the game are known.

Likeness to Truth

Peter Bernstein was an economist and money manager who began his investment career in 1951. I have read many of his writings and had the privilege of meeting him over a decade ago. In 2009, he was scheduled to speak at a conference I was attending, but unfortunately he passed away at the age of 90 before he had the opportunity to take the podium one last time.

Mr. Bernstein wrote these words of wisdom of which, I believe, all individual investors should take heed:

"Likeness to truth is not the same as truth. Without theoretical structure to explain why patterns seem to repeat themselves across time or across systems, these innovations provide little assurance that today's signals will trigger tomorrow's events. We are left with only the subtle sequences of data that the enormous power of the computer can reveal."[40]

Financial markets have only one past and continually revisiting it until you find a formula for creating wealth will eventually produce something that looks viable, but remember the standard disclaimer of the financial advice industry:

"Past performance is no guarantee of future performance."

CHAPTER 4

FINANCIAL MARKETS SUPPOSITIONS

"And finally, no matter how good the science gets, there are problems that inevitably depend on judgment, on art, on a feel for financial markets."

Martin Feldstein, economist

Financial market news is ever present in your daily life. It appears on the internet and in print news every day. It will usually be the lead headline every time an index reaches a new high or a new low. There are television channels dedicated to providing financial market information and you have access to instant stock prices by simply pressing a button on your smart phone.

What Is The Stock Market?

In exchange for cash, corporations issue shares of stock to investors to raise capital for investments. This issued stock represents a proportional ownership of a company's assets and its profits. Companies list their shares on stock exchanges (*the stock market*), so that investors can buy and sell the shares in an easily accessible forum. The majority of buying and selling of shares is concentrated on the exchanges; it allows the price that investors are willing to pay for a share to be known every second of each day that the exchange is open for trading.

The term stock market is usually interchangeable as a reference to a *stock market index* such as the S&P/TSX Composite Index. These broad market averages are based on both the total market value and price performance of the shares of each company that are included in the index. Indexes are designed as a benchmark to inform investors how shares that are traded on the stock market are performing on average.

As I discussed in the section regarding the law of large numbers, a valuation of each company's shares can be determined by estimating the current and future cash flows of the company that are available to shareholders. These cash flows are then discounted by a risk adjusted interest rate to determine an estimated present value. Therefore, the current price of a stock reflects the dividend that the stock currently pays, the projected future earnings of the company, and some type of multiple that investors are willing to pay for the right to own these cash flows.

Financial markets have been in existence since the 1300s as a means for investors to trade various types of debt and early forms of securities that were similar to what we consider stocks. Since these early beginnings, analysts and investors have attempted to develop models or methods that would predict returns and future prices. Philosophers, astronomers, physicists, mathematicians and traders have all made attempts to develop theories that would allow them to find an "investment holy grail".

Over the centuries these models have changed and evolved as the performance of financial markets eventually proved them to be inaccurate, which subsequently lead to the development of the next new theory that was accepted by investors as being *correct*. This is a repetitive cycle that will continue for as long as financial markets exist.

Since the 1950s, the accepted theories have focused on the Efficient Market Theory and Modern Portfolio Theory. They are widely referenced in academic research, are taught at business schools and as part of the Chartered Financial Analyst program.

Financial Markets as Efficient

The Efficient Market Hypothesis states that stock prices already reflect all known information concerning a security and that prices will rapidly adjust to any new information. Information is not limited to what is currently known about a security, but also any future expectations, such as changes to earnings growth or dividend payments.

The foundation of the Efficient Market Hypothesis is the belief that financial markets consist of many rational investors, who are constantly receiving information and then reacting quickly so that it is reflected in the price of securities.

The Efficient Market Hypothesis is based on following constructs:

- Information is widely available to all investors.

- Investors use this information to analyze individual securities and to make investment decisions.

- Events that have a major impact on security prices are generally unpredictable.

- Individual investors will react quickly to any new information and adjust their perceived value of a security.

A theory regarding the efficiency of financial markets was first expressed in 1900 by the French mathematician Louis Bachelier (The Theory of Speculation). However, his work was largely ignored until the Efficient Market Theory was developed by Eugene Fama in 1970. Fama published a paper that extended and refined the theory and provided evidence to support the hypothesis. The paper outlined three forms of market efficiency, based on what information is embedded in security prices:

- In the weak form, only past market trading information, such as prices and volume, are considered. This implies that technical analysis, which relies exclusively on past trading data to forecast future price movements, is useless.

- The semi-strong form includes past market trading information, but also includes publicly available information, such as news and earning announcements. This implies that fundamental analysis, which relies on projecting the future earnings and dividends of a company, is useless.

- The strong form extends the information further to include not only past and public information, but also private information. This is information known by officers and executives of the corporation. This means that even corporate "insiders" cannot make abnormal profits by trading their company's stock before they release corporate information to the public.

The Efficient Market Theory is founded on the belief that markets are *information-ally efficient*. Therefore, no investor will consistently be able to achieve risk-adjusted returns in excess of that of the average market return, since all information that could affect security prices is already available at the time any investment is made.

Modern Portfolio Theory

Modern Portfolio Theory was developed by Harry Markowitz in the 1950s and is the conceptual foundation for the benefit of using diversification when investing. The theory was also considered an important advance in the ability to use mathematical models in finance.

The theory is based on the premise that investing is a trade-off between risk and return. Investments which have higher expected returns are generally riskier. Modern Portfolio Theory attempts to maximize the expected return of a portfolio for a specific amount of portfolio risk.

To maximize the benefits of diversification, investments in a portfolio should not be selected individually. Instead, it is more important to consider how each investment changes in price relative to how every other investment in the portfolio also changes in price.

The theory also assumes that individual investors are risk averse. This implies that when presented with two portfolios that offer the same expected return, you will prefer the less risky one. Therefore, you will only take on increased risk if you are compensated by higher expected returns. You will also evaluate the risk/return trade-off based on your own individual risk tolerance and, as a rational investor, you will not invest in one portfolio if another portfolio exists with a more favourable risk/reward opportunity.

Modern Portfolio Theory considers *risk* to be the price volatility of investments that can result in a possible loss of capital. The Theory defines two types of risk:

- Specific Risk, which is the volatility associated with individual investments.

- Systematic Risk, which is volatility that cannot be eliminated through diversification.

Specific risk is diversifiable. Within a portfolio this type of risk can be reduced through diversification, as the specific risks of each investment can offset the others. As a result, an investor can reduce investment risk simply by holding combinations of investments that are not positively correlated (meaning that security prices will not move in the same direction at the same time). Any investment pairs that have correlations of 0 are perfectly uncorrelated. Therefore, an investor can reduce exposure to individual asset risk by holding a diversified portfolio of uncorrelated investments.

Systematic risk cannot be eliminated through diversification. It refers to overall market risk and would include such risks as: interest rate risk, exchange rate risk, and events that affect the entire market. Modern Portfolio Theory conceives that this type of risk can be measured mathematically. The measurement is done by using a normal statistical distribution and the standard deviation of the returns of a portfolio.

Math Warning (But Understanding These Concepts Are Important)

The *Bell Curve* is the popular name for a normal statistical distribution. It is called the bell curve because the graph of its probability distribution resembles a bell shape. A normal distribution of data infers that most of the observations in a set of data are close to the "average", while relatively few observations tend to be at one extreme or the other.

Standard deviation (the measure of the width of the distribution) is a statistic that shows how tightly all the various observations are clustered around the mean (located at the center of the curve) in a set of data. Not all sets of data will have graphs that look like a perfect bell shape. When the observations are tightly bunched together and the curve is steep, the standard deviation is small. When the observations are more widely spread apart and the curve is relatively flat, the standard deviation is large.

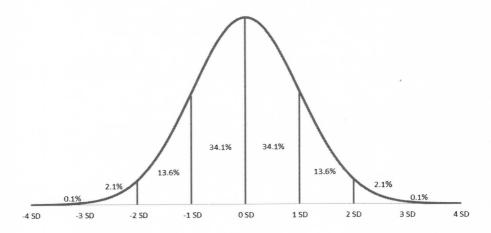

The above graph illustrates a normal bell curve distribution. One standard deviation away from the mean in either direction on the horizontal axis accounts for just over 68% of the observations. Two standard deviations away from the mean will account for roughly 95% of the observations, and three standard deviations account for about 99% of the observations.

Modern Portfolio Theory assumes that returns from an investment portfolio occur like a normal distribution. Most return observations are near the mean of the distribution, while observations near the sides (called tails) are unusual or rare.

Eloquent Foundations, But Full of Cracks...

Both of todays accepted theories of financial markets are founded on the assumptions that:

- Financial market returns are normally distributed.

- Price changes of securities are statistically independent.

- Investors are rational when making their investment decisions.

By using statistical measurements of variability like standard deviation and the correlations of different securities, investors can evaluate investment portfolios by their risk probability and then create an efficient portfolio to target a specific return with a desired level of risk.

The theories are very eloquent and they seem to fit neatly into mathematical models, but like all foundations they eventually begin to show cracks...

Crack #1

Individuals Are Risk Adverse

Modern Portfolio Theory contains the assumption that individuals are *always* risk adverse. Therefore, when you are confronted with a choice between either a sure bet, or a bet with a less certain outcome that also has the same economic payoff, you will always choose the sure bet.

Risk tolerance is a psychological trait, as are intelligence, personality, attitude and values. For that reason, the concept of risk will differ among individuals. It could mean danger or uncertainty to you, but it can also mean opportunity or thrill to someone else. Individuals react differently to risk, but do they consistently react to all risky decisions in exactly the same way? Will you habitually reject risk in all situations, while I am predisposed to always accepting it?

In reality, your decisions will be a mixture of risk avoidance as well as risk seeking behaviour (think: you purchase both lottery tickets and life insurance).

Your decisions will be affected by the variety of uncertain circumstances that are present when you make a decision and by what is motivating you to take a risk.

Your preference for either risk seeking or risk avoidance has been found to be related to such desires as control, achievement, ambiguity avoidance, or thrill seeking. If you make a risky choice that is motivated by your need for achievement, it will differ from a risky choice that is motivated by a need to experience a thrill. In the first example, the risky choice serves as an *instrument* to reach a particular economic goal in the future. In the second example, the risky choice is a source of strong and immediate emotional excitement. These two distinct forms of risk taking have been labelled *instrumental risk taking* and *stimulating risk taking*.[41]

How you make risk taking decisions is based on your basic intentions that stimulate the risk taking. When you accept instrumental risk in an attempt to achieve a future goal, you strive for controlling the environment to avoid the possibility of engaging in an activity where the outcome depends mainly on chance. Therefore, an instrumental risk decision will involve deliberation about the various possible consequences, analysis of any numerical probabilities and assessing the potential undesirable outcomes. An instrumental risk decision is achievement orientated and based on the complex way of information processing that is used by your logical brain.

A stimulating risk taking decision will come from your automatic brain and it will unconsciously produce a physiological reaction that is connected with the risky decision. Whether the reaction is pleasant or unpleasant will either motivate you to seek more of the same, or avoid another unpleasant reaction in the future.

Consider the following example of Sally and Simon, who are seated beside each other at a blackjack table in a casino. This is the first time that Sally has ever entered a casino. Until today she has never placed a bet on a game of cards. However, she only has $100 and she desperately needs $1000 by tomorrow to pay her rent. She does not like gambling, but she believes that this is the only way to get the money she needs. Simon goes to the casino every weekend. He loves the excitement of watching the cards turn to see if he is a winner. He also has $100, but he considers potentially losing this money as his "admission cost" for receiving his gambling thrill.

Sally and Simon are taking the same economic risk today with their $100, but would you expect that they will continue to make the same risky decision choices in the future?

It's likely that once Sally's motivation to change her current circumstances through making a stimulating risk choice is over, she will then revert to her preference to continue to be risk adverse by making only instrumental risk decisions. Simon will continue to be risk seeking and continue to make stimulating risk decisions.

This example shows that you can be risk averse in some situations, but risk seeking in others. Your *perception* of risk can change when your personal circumstances are altered, or you are presented with new information.

In chapter two I discussed loss aversion and Prospect Theory. Prospect Theory shows that individuals value gains and losses differently and will also base their decisions on perceived gains rather than perceived losses. As a result, if an individual is given two equal choices, one expressed in terms of possible gains and the other in possible losses, the individual will choose the former even if they provide the same monetary result.

To your detriment, in many circumstances you are willing to assume a higher level of risk in order to avoid the emotional pain of loss (think: loss aversion). Prospect Theory further reinforces how your perception of risk is not consistent and will be influenced by the circumstances and reference points in which you are making your risk taking decision.

A basis for the accepted theories of financial markets is rational decision making by individual investors, but can this always occur, given the heuristic biases we all possess?

Crack #2

All Investors Have Access to the Same Information at the Same Time

Equal access to information forms part of the basis for the Efficient Market Theory, but the realities of modern financial markets and technology makes this difficult to accept. There always has been and always will be discrepancies in how quickly information is obtained by various types of investors. In the simplest terms, corporate insiders will always have access to information regarding their companies before this news is disseminated to the investing public. For this reason, securities laws make it illegal for them to profit from what they know.

Even among investors who are not corporate insiders, there are just some individuals and institutions that are better informed than others. This occurs because, in practice, access to information actually encompasses a wide range of costs, which can include not only the actual dollars spent, but also the time and effort required to read, process and analyze this information.

The media now has a large and growing market for their coverage of financial markets and the internet has improved access to information and low-cost trading. Prior to 1995, internet trading did not exist and real-time financial market information was mostly accessible only to financial institutions. Basic transactional and information services have now become commoditized and increasingly compete solely on the basis of price.

Investors can now search the internet for commentary, subscribe to newsletters, read brokerage research reports, or perform their own analysis. However, obtaining relevant and quality information in this universe of reports and opinions is a daunting task.

The rise of the internet and the consolidation of financial market exchanges have literally created a 24 hour, borderless, global trading environment. Technology has shrunk the world and reduced the importance of the geographical location of financial markets. Advances in telecommunications and information processing now offer financial institutions the capability to handle vast amount of data, at very high speed and at relatively low costs. Although technology has reduced information asymmetry to some degree, the access-to-information playing field is not entirely level.

Many factors can affect the amount of time it takes for information to travel over the internet, including network congestion, the size of the electronic information packet and the speed at which the receiving systems process information.

Some financial exchanges also offer services that provide clients a faster look at quotations, in exchange for a fee. As a result, some investors receive access to information sooner than others who rely on more standard services.

And this is the rub, the access to information and the technology required to process it, always has a cost. Institutions can more readily afford to pay for this information than most individual investors. Even among individual investors, studies have shown that expenditures to access information increases with income. Donkers and Van Soest (1997) used a survey sample to show that interest in financial matters is strongly and positively correlated to household income. The result is that the more money you have available to invest, the more you also have to spend on obtaining information.[42]

The ability to pay for superior access to information is a well-known fact in the financial marketplace. Take, for instance, the Institute for Supply Management's (ISM) Chicago Purchasing Manager Index (PMI). This survey is widely considered to be a leading indicator of U.S. economic activity. In fact, the ISM website uses the following quote:

"The ISM-Chicago Business Survey, a regional view of the national economy, is a time-tested, market-moving report."[43]

The ISM Chicago PMI is also available to subscribers three minutes before its release to the public on the last working day each month.

Yahoo! Finance is one of largest financial information sites available on the internet and is frequently used by individual investors as a means to obtain access to corporate news releases. An analysis of 100 company news releases shows that the average delay between when wire services release the information to financial institution subscribers and when most investors actually have access to it on Yahoo! Finance is just over 83 seconds. Even though 83 seconds may appear to be a small delay, in an investment environment of almost instant electronic trading, company news is routinely the trigger of heavy trading and 83 seconds can mean the difference between profit and loss.[44]

In the days before modern technology began to dominate the financial markets, being as close as possible to the action in a trading pit was how traders got the best prices and overheard the best information.

Although technology has improved, the compulsion to be close to the action has not changed. The introduction of co-location, or proximity hosting, allows brokerage firms to physically place their computer servers as close as metres away from those of a market exchange, with the goal of reducing the transmission time required to send electronic trading instructions. Financial market exchanges now offer space in custom-built facilities to reduce the time it takes to execute a trade to a millisecond. The result is that these firms can utilize much faster, high-frequency trading strategies.

Many exchanges in North America, Europe and Asia offer these co-location facilities. The TMX Group, which is the operator of the Toronto Stock Exchange, has a facility with 200 co-location spaces allowing connections to its equities and derivatives platforms simultaneously.

Even if we ignore the ability to pay for information, or the fact that some investors will always have superior technology, when it comes to financial markets it is inevitable someone will always have some facts first.

Accessibility discrepancies are present not only with the speed at which various types of investors obtain information, but also depending on whether some types of information is even available to all market participants.

Information regarding any security that is traded on a financial exchange is transparent, since the current price and past history of these transactions is widely available. However, there are large classes of securities where basic information availability is, at best, opaque and, at worst, not disclosed at all.

A derivative is a contract between two parties, where the value of the contract is *derived* from the price of an underlying asset. The underlying asset could be a physical commodity, an interest rate, a company's stock, an index or a currency.

The terms of the contract are designed to transfer the risk associated with a change in price of the underlying asset between the parties of the contract.

There are two broad categories of derivative contracts that are distinguished by the way in which the contracts are traded:

- Contracts that are traded on exchanges. These types of contracts are generically known as options and futures.

- Over-the-counter (OTC) contracts that are bilateral, privately-negotiated agreements. These types of contracts are generically known as swaps and forwards.

Exchange listed and OTC derivative contracts have some key differences:

The terms of an exchange listed contract are standardized for each type of contract. For an OTC contract, all terms are subject to negotiation by the parties to the contract.

An exchange listed contract is always traded on an exchange, while OTC contracts are traded on a *best efforts* bilateral basis.

An exchange listed contract has an intermediary or clearinghouse, which guarantees that the terms of the contact will be met. Parties to an OTC contract are exposed to the risk that a counterparty may not live up to its contractual obligations. This is often referred to as *counterparty risk*. An exchange traded contract is subject to default mitigation measures such as margin requirements. These types of measures can be optional for OTC contracts.

Let's Swap Risk

Let's review an example of how an interest rate swap works:

- The notional value is $1 million.

- The term of the contract is three years.

Party A agrees to pay party B a fixed rate of 4%. Party A receives from Party B, the 3-month Treasury Bill rate plus 2%.

Why would both parties enter into this type of contract?

Party A has an initial position in a fixed rate debt instrument, while Party B has an initial position in a floating rate obligation. In this initial position, Party B with the floating rate obligation is exposed to upward increases in interest rates. Therefore, by swapping this floating rate obligation, the interest rate swap decreases Party B's risk to rising interest rates.

Party A pays 4% of $1 million, or $40,000 each year to Party B. Party B makes a payment to Party A in return, but the actual amount of the payments depends on movement in Treasury Bill rates. Party A would profit from a belief that short-term interest rates were going to rise substantially over the next three years. However, if the short-term rate falls, Party A will lose on this derivative contract. These differing views and outcomes are always present in financial markets.

Despite a notional value of $1 million for the contract, this notional amount is not exchanged by the parties. Instead, the parties transfer the net payments based upon the contract's terms.

What Does A Private Contract Have To Do With Financial Markets?

The OTC derivatives market began in the early 1980s and has grown into one of the largest sectors of financial markets. This growth has occurred despite OTC derivative contracts not having:

- Standardized terms.

- Liquid trading markets.

- A clearinghouse that guarantees the terms of contracts.

- Margin requirements to mitigate default risk.

- Direct regulation.

Given the private nature of OTC contracts, it is difficult to obtain an accurate estimate of the total size of outstanding contract values. However, in June 2010, the Bank for International Settlements estimates that OTC contracts total $583 trillion compared to exchange listed contracts of $114 trillion. To put this number in perspective, the market capitalization of all the companies traded on U.S. stock exchanges is approximately $55 trillion.[45]

This total value estimate of the OTC derivative market is based on notional values, which are the underlying asset values that the contracts are based upon. Supporters of the use of derivatives accurately point out that the actual economic exposure of the parties is less than these amounts. This occurs because, unlike a bond or debenture, derivatives transactions do not involve payments of principal amounts. Instead they require periodic payments based on the underlying notional amounts, but not payments of the notional values themselves.

In the previous example of a swap for a variable interest rate in exchange for a 4% fixed rate on a $1 million notional value, it is required that the parties make annual payments with each other of $40,000 or less. Future payments will be adjusted depending on how interest rates change. Neither party to the swap risks $1 million.

However, the notional value becomes relevant if either counterparty to the OTC derivative contract defaults. Counterparty risk is the weak link in the chain of the derivatives market. If any one party defaults, then the risk that the other party believed was offset by the contract now reappears. Whether the default is a one-off event or a multiple event, such as the bankruptcy of a major OTC derivative dealer, can have major repercussions for financial markets. The bankruptcy of a major dealer would begin a cascade of time dependent defaults among counterparties.

The high level of concentration that exists among derivatives dealers and the international linkages of these dealers further heighten counterparty risk. According to the International Swap Dealers Association (ISDA), in 2010 the fourteen largest derivatives dealers held 82% of the total notional amount of outstanding OTC contracts. Categorized by contract type, these 14 dealers held 82% of interest rate derivatives, 90% of credit default swaps, and 86% of equity derivatives. Therefore, a failure or withdrawal from a market of one of these major dealers would likely have a negative effect on the solvency of the remaining dealers.[46]

The information advantage that these dealers have over other market participants is enormous. Only the dealers know the terms of the contracts that they have entered into on their own behalf, but they also know the terms of the contracts that their customers have completed when the dealer acted as a broker to execute the contract. The dealer knows both the terms and also how much the customer paid to execute the contract. Therefore, they have privileged access to information about how specific market events may affect another market participant.

The opaque nature of OTC derivative contracts and dealer conflicts are prime examples of how what you don't know *can* hurt you in financial markets.

Crack #3

Correlations Between Assets are Always Fixed and Constant

Financial market history has shown that the perceived diversification benefits of investment correlations can break down or change. The 2008 equity market experience illustrated how these breakdowns frequently occur at the most inopportune times, because during periods of financial crisis all assets tend to become positively correlated and move lower together. Therefore, the benefits of diversification, on which Modern Portfolio Theory is based, break down when individual investors are most in need of the protection.

Why does this happen?

Correlation measures both the strength and the direction of a linear relationship between two variables. An increasingly negative correlation indicates an inverse relationship. Correlation is measured numerically between +1 to -1, where -1 indicates a perfect inverse relationship and +1 indicates a perfect positive relation-ship. Therefore, if two investments had a perfect correlation their prices would be expected to increase and decrease in an equal fixed proportion over a certain period of time.

This concept is simple enough, but individual investors must also understand what correlation cannot provide.

Despite the fact that correlation calculations are based on *past* historical relation-ships between investments, investors rely on this past data to frame their expectations for a future time horizon. The assumption of investors and Modern Portfolio Theory is that correlations will remain constant over time. In reality, many investment cor-relations frequently shift significantly and unexpectedly. Since measured correlations can be volatile, this is often to the detriment of a portfolio that was believed to be adequately diversified.

Correlation differences actually have a more modest diversification benefit than many individual investors perceive. In fact, in the case of combining stocks and bonds, the single largest factor contributing to the decline in portfolio volatility arises from the lower total volatility of bonds, not the fact that stocks and bonds have low correlation.

The chart below shows the 5-year correlations between monthly U.S. stock and U.S. bond total returns over 5-year intervals since 1926 (16 separate non overlapping periods). While the long-term average correlation between these two asset classes has been 0.26, the chart shows that correlations over shorter periods will vary widely from this average, with a range of 0.75 for the 5-year period ended 1975 to –0.54 for the 5-year period ended 2005.

Dopel (2003) examined the correlation between the returns of U.S. stocks and U.S. bonds that is typically assumed to be a constant value between 0.30 and 0.50 during 36-month rolling time horizons. His examination of correlations from 1929 through June 2003 shows four periods where the correlation was negative. In fact, the correlation between the returns from stocks and bonds was negative for a full 10-year period, averaging -0.23 from 1955 to 1964.[47]

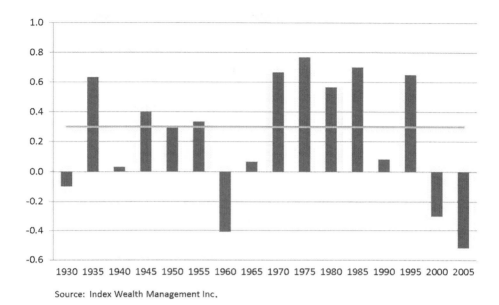

Source: Index Wealth Management Inc.

During a financial panic, the quality and liquidity of investments becomes the primary concern of investors as the increased level of systematic risk (think: non-diversifiable risk) tends to dominate asset-specific risk. The result is that many types of investments have a tendency to suddenly become more positively correlated, often in contrast with how they perform during periods of normal market volatility.[48]

The fluctuation of observed correlations can be caused by either:

- Historical correlation relationships that are actually breaking down.

- Simple randomness in the pattern of the investment returns.

Both factors will produce outcomes that differ from a longer-term average, when measured over shorter time periods. Since correlation is a property of random variables, correlations among investments will vary over both time and different circumstances. Even assets with past low and unchanging correlation can, and will, move in the same direction from time to time. Future correlations may also differ from those in the past, due to the constant evolution of financial market environments.

Low historical and estimated future correlations do not insure against loss. Therefore, when assessing the value of diversification, beware of placing too much faith in the future replicating the past.

Crack #4

Financial Market Returns Resemble Those of a Bell Curve

Remember that standard deviation is the statistical measure that shows how tightly all the various observations in a distribution are clustered around the mean. The larger the variation of the points in the data, the higher the standard deviation. A low standard deviation indicates that the data points tend to be very close to the mean, whereas a high standard deviation indicates that the data is spread out over a large range of values.

Under the normal statistical distribution of the bell curve, deviations from the mean return should occur with a certain frequency. The larger the size of a deviation, the lower should be its frequency of occurrence. Modern Portfolio Theory uses the standard deviation investment of returns as the measure of the risk of the investment. Returns within one standard deviation away from the mean should capture just over 68% of the observations. Returns within two standard deviations away from the mean will include roughly 95% of the observations, and returns within three standard deviations will account for about 99% of the observations.

The probabilities of exceeding multiples of standard deviation in a normal bell curve distribution are:

> 0 SD: 1 in 2 times
>
> 1 SD: 1 in 6.3 times
>
> 2 SD: 1 in 44 times
>
> 3 SD: 1 in 740 times
>
> 4 SD: 1 in 32,000 times
>
> 5 SD: 1 in 3,500,000 times

6 SD: 1 in 1,000,000,000 times

7 SD: 1 in 780,000,000,000 times

8 SD: 1 in 1,600,000,000,000,000 times

9 SD: 1 in 8,900,000,000,000,000,000 times

10 SD: 1 in 130,000,000,000,000,000,000, 000 times

Therefore, a return that is 6 standard deviations from the mean should only occur about 1 in 1,000,000,000 times. It should be incredibly rare; so rare in fact, that very few individual investors will ever need to worry about experiencing its impact. However, this assumption of rarity is not correct.

The table below shows the daily performance of the S&P 500 Stock Index from 1923 to 2009. The first S&P index was introduced in 1923 and consisted of 90 companies. In 1957, the number of companies included in the index was expanded to 500. This index is considered to be a broad representation of U.S. stock market performance.

The data in the table shows that the actual distribution of the market returns differs significantly from what would be expected if the returns were normally distributed as assumed by Modern Portfolio Theory. Worse still, the normal distribution underestimates the probability of having very significant negative returns. If risk is about losing money, then these are the days that matter to you.

I would define significant negative days as being four or more standard deviations from the mean. As an example, the normal distribution of the daily return of the S&P 500 Index would suggest that a negative three standard deviation event (-3.5% daily return) should have occurred 27 times over the last one hundred years. However, a daily decline of this magnitude has actually occurred 100 times in the 81 years since 1927.

The results are even more startling when you look at more extreme negative days. The expected likelihood of a negative four standard deviation event (-4.7% daily return) is once in one hundred years; yet a decline of this magnitude has occurred 43 times since 1927.

S&P 500 Daily Return Data—Actual vs. Expected Normal Distribution

# of SD from Mean	Observed	Expected
6 SD	26	0
5 SD	13	0
4 SD	34	1
3 SD	89	27
2 SD	276	435
1 SD	1393	2761
0	16604	13872
(1 SD)	1377	2761
(2 SD)	325	435
(3 SD)	100	27
(4 SD)	43	1
(5 SD)	19	0
(6 SD)	21	0
Total	20320	20320

Source: Bloomberg

The normal bell curve distribution also predicts essentially no realistic probability (.00003%) of a day where a negative return is experienced greater than -5.8%. These are negative five and six standard deviation events. However, on 40 days in the last 81 years, investors in this market have experienced these *improbable* declines. In 2008, declines of this size were experienced three times alone.

These very large single day declines also tend to occur unevenly over time, meaning that volatility tends to cluster. During the period of 1930 to 1939, when the U.S. economy suffered through the Great Depression, there was a higher occurrence of these extreme single day events.

There were six days between 1920 and 1940 when the market experienced declines of six standard deviations. The market then advanced for four decades without experiencing any nerve rattling declines. Memories of these declines were then eventually forgotten by most financial market participants (think: representativeness bias).

Then, without warning, the new granddaddy of market rattling events occurred on October 19th, 1987. Black Monday was a 22 standard deviation event with a 20.47% decline.

Date	S&P 500 Index Daily Return
10/19/1987	-20.47%
10/28/1929	-12.94%
10/29/1929	-10.16%
11/06/1929	-9.92%
09/03/1946	-9.91%
10/18/1937	-9.12%
10/05/1931	-9.07%
10/15/2008	-9.03%
07/20/1933	-8.88%
09/29/2008	-8.79%
07/21/1933	-8.88%
09/29/2008	-8.79%
07/21/1933	-8.70%
10/10/1932	-8.55%
10/26/1987	-8.28%
10/05/1932	-8.02%
07/26/1934	-7.83%
06/16/1930	-7.64%
10/09/2008	-7.62%
05/14/1940	-7.47%
05/31/1932	-7.45%
09/24/1931	-7.29%

Source: Bloomberg

In 2008, the market experienced another period of extreme volatility as subprime mortgage and collateralized debt securities threatened the stability of the global financial system. That year ended with the dubious distinction of being the only year with a greater frequency of extreme single day declines other than 1932.

When equity market returns are compared to those expected from a normal bell curve distribution, historical data has shown a <u>significantly larger degree of uncertainty</u> in the daily returns of the S&P 500 Index.

In reality, financial market returns more closely resemble Leptokurtic distributions. Compared to a bell curve these types of distributions have:

- A more acute peak that produces a lower probability of values near the mean.

- Larger tails that produce a higher probability of extreme values.

These larger tails are often referred to as *fat tails*. Leptokurtic distributions have lower standard deviations than bell curve distributions, which provide a false statistical sense of stability until the next wild occurrence in the tails of the distribution appears. As a result, the relative *rarity* of an extreme event, lulls you into underestimating the dangers of it occurring.

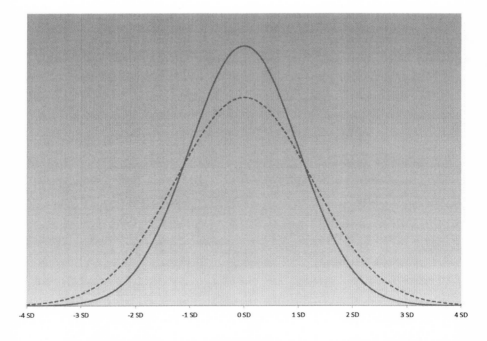

Don't be fooled. In financial markets, literally anything is possible and will eventually occur.

Crack #5

Investors' Actions Do Not Influence Security Prices

Liquidity refers to the ability to purchase or sell a security without causing a significant change in the price when a trade is executed. A perfectly liquid security will allow for the next trade to be equal in price to the previous one. Volume measures how often a security is traded. The *depth* of a market for a security can be measured by the number of shares that can be purchased or sold at a given price before a price change is required to complete the next trade. Therefore, a key characteristic of a liquid financial market is that there must be an abundance of buyers and sellers at all times in order to create depth.

Modern Portfolio Theory assumes that financial markets are *frictionless,* so an individual investor can purchase any amount of securities that are needed to construct a diversified portfolio without having these actions influence the prices of the securities.

In an efficient financial market all securities with the same cash flows and the same perceived risk must have the same price. Otherwise investors could purchase the less expensive security and simultaneously sell the more expensive security, and receive unlimited risk free arbitrage profits. Therefore, if financial markets are plagued by forms of illiquidity, then another main premise of Efficient Market Theory is suspect.

In actuality, changes in liquidity occur in financial markets as the consequence of not all potential investors being present in a market at all times. For example, a seller of a security may not be present in a market when a buyer wants to purchase at a desired price level. This imbalance in supply and demand will result in a change in price until it reaches a point that present buyers and sellers will now execute the trade. Large purchases of individual securities frequently shift market prices not only for the security that was purchased, but also for other securities that may be related to it. Therefore, there are periods when an individual investor may not be able to assemble a reasonably priced and properly diversified portfolio, or may not be able to rebalance a portfolio to allow it to remain optimal.

Liquidity in financial markets is complex. It is continually influenced by factors that affect the entire market and by security specific factors. Changes in both types of these liquidity factors can create unexpected consequences for individual investors.[49]

- Entire market liquidity (Exogenous) affects all investors present in a market, and is not influenced by the actions of any single investor. This implies a liquid market for most securities that would be characterized by large daily trading volumes and continuous depth across most price levels. An illiquid market would typically have both volatile depth and trading volumes. An individual investor accepts this type of illiquidity risk by choosing which broad asset class of securities in which to invest (think: domestic equities or foreign equities).

- Security specific liquidity (Endogenous) is specific to each individual investor's investments. It will vary across all investors, but the exposure to this type of illiquidity risk is affected by an investor's own unique investment decisions. (think: a junior mining company or a bank). Frequently, this type of illiquidity risk will also increase in proportion to the size of an investment.

There's a Hole in the Market

Liquidity in any security, sector, or market is not constant. Both general market and security specific illiquidity risk will vary over time as investors react to new information.

Financial market history is punctuated with many periods of extreme turbulence. These periods are characterized by seemingly endless waves of sell orders for many securities that overwhelm all potential buyers and result in rapid price changes. These periods are often called *liquidity holes*. The analogy comes from the visual image of many objects trying to squeeze through a small hole simultaneously (think: cattle pushing through a small open gate in a coral). These periods are not just characterized by rapid price changes, they also produce their own momentum from the combined influence of risk reduction decisions by many individual investors (think: herding).[50]

Liquidity holes are produced by the feedback individual investors receive through observing the investment decisions that are being made by other investors. In many circumstances, when asset prices begin to fall only some investors will initially sell to limit their losses. New buyers appear at these lower price levels that they perceive to be bargains. This is viewed as normal market movement; some days markets move higher and some days they move lower. However, in a liquidity hole environment this selling pressure begins a cycle of more pronounced downward pressure on asset prices, as the automatic brains of investors begin to make investment decisions. The *pain* of the recent declines (think: loss aversion and representativeness bias) becomes more important than long-term investment goals. Losses follow more losses and the cycle appears endless (think: availability bias) which induces more selling and the withdrawal of potential buyers. The market turbulence seems like it will never end and then, without warning, just as it began, the turbulences subsides and eventually reverses direction.

Some of these liquidity hole events can be attributed to the large and growing ownership of equities by institutions (think: pension funds and mutual funds) as opposed to individual investors. U.S. institutional investors have increased their ownership of U.S. equity markets substantially: rising from 37.2% of total U.S. equities in 1980 to 61.2% of total U.S. equities in 2005.[51]

Many traders for institutional organizations have restrictions on their behaviour that limit their investment decision making ability. These controls, such as daily loss limits, restrict the discretion of traders and are sometimes referred to as *VAR* or *value at risk* controls.

These limits are strictly loss dependent and are not based on an opinion of the security's perceived value. They instead are an attempt to limit the risk profile of the institution's overall investment portfolio. When a loss limit is reached and a security position must be sold, this tends to accelerate the losses of already declining security prices. Although the loss limits across traders will differ, institutions with similar investment objectives will frequently have large investments in the same securities (think: security specific illiquidity risk). These forced sales then become correlated with other institutions that have similar risk factors in their portfolios. This increases the incentives for other traders to sell and every sale becomes self-reinforcing.

LTCM

Long-Term Capital Management (LTCM) was a hedge fund founded by John Meriwether, Nobel Prize winning economists Myron Scholes and Robert Merton, and David Mullins, a former vice-chairman of the Federal Reserve Board who resigned to become a partner at LTCM.

LTCM's main investment strategy was to make *convergence* trades in government bonds. Since government bonds pay a fixed amount of interest at specified times in the future, the price difference between a security with 24½ years to maturity and one with 25 years to maturity, should not be that significant. However, small discrepancies in price between these two bonds can arise because of differences in liquidity between similar bonds. Some bonds will have more market depth because they are used as benchmarks and therefore are priced at levels that are more expensive than the bonds that are traded less frequently. Convergence trades are designed to simultaneously purchase the less expensive 24 ½-year bond and *sell short* (selling a borrowed security with the intention of purchasing it in the future at a lower price) the more expensive, but more liquid, 25-year bond. These trading pairs were projected to become profitable as the prices eventually converged when the bonds moved closer to the maturity dates.

Since the price differences of the bond trading pairs were very small, LTCM needed to take extremely large and highly *leveraged* positions in order to make a significant profit. Leverage involves borrowing money to increase the size of an investment, while using the investment security itself as collateral for the loan. At the beginning of 1998, LTCM had capital from investors of $5 billion and had borrowed over $125 billion, which is a leverage factor of roughly thirty to one! LTCM models based on past market history showed that their bond trading pairs were strongly positively correlated, so the fund managers believed that the risk they were taking was controllable, despite the incredible sum of money they had borrowed.[52]

According to the Efficient Market Theory, two bonds with identical risk should sell for the same price, otherwise investors can make risk free arbitrage profits. This was exactly what the portfolio managers at LTCM believed they were achieving. However, in real market environments investors are also concerned about the liquidity of their investments. In some circumstances, they are willing to pay a premium price to hold more liquid assets and this premium will change with the degree of urgency investors develop to own liquid investments.

In August 1998, Russia unexpectedly devalued its currency and simultaneously declared a moratorium on paying interest on its debt. The result was a sudden re-evaluation of the risk by investors who held bonds issued by emerging market governments. A liquidity hole resulted in global bond markets, with investors trying to sell securities that were suddenly risky and replace them with securities that they perceived as more secure.

In times of financial market turbulence, U.S. Treasury bonds are viewed as the most secure and most liquid investment asset class. This time was no different and a flood of new investment dollars rushed into the treasury market. The large majority of these new purchases were directed primarily to the most liquid treasury bonds available in the market. As investors squeezed through the liquidity hole and purchased these liquid treasury bonds, the prices of the securities that LTCM viewed as expensive and sold short, became even more expensive. The price spread between the most liquid treasury securities and less liquid securities increased dramatically, resulting in LTCM's trading pairs moving in the opposite direction than was predicted by the models (think: correlations are not constant).

Since LTCM's pair trades were declining in value, this meant that the hedge fund had less collateral to support the massive amount of money that it had borrowed to increase its leverage. LTCM's lenders began to force the fund to liquidate a number of its investments at exactly the most unfavourable time for pricing of these trading pairs. A cycle of losses producing more losses (think: herding and availability bias) overwhelmed global fixed income markets (think: fat tails).

On September 23, 1998 the Federal Reserve Bank of New York and several major brokerage firms announced a bailout package. LTCM's equity tumbled from $2.3 billion at the start of September to $400 million on September 25th. The total losses in the fund would eventually be $4.6 billion. For readers who enjoy irony, two of the brokerage firms that assisted in the bailout (Merrill Lynch and Salomon Smith Barney) were themselves also bankrupted in 2008 by the liquidity hole that occurred in the U.S. real estate collateralized debt obligations (CDO) and credit default swaps (CDS).

As large as LTCM was, it was only one fund. Why was a bailout of a single hedge fund so important to the Federal Reserve and the financial markets?

LTCM was a client of, and also owed leverage loans to, nearly all the major brokerage firms in the U.S. As LTCM began to fail, there was a belief that the failure could cause a chain reaction in numerous markets, causing catastrophic losses throughout the financial system. How could that occur?

Since institutions that have similar risk factors in their portfolios will frequently have large investments in the same securities (think: security specific illiquidity risk), so almost all of the investors who were using leveraged Treasury bond strategies held similar positions to LTCM. Therefore, LTCM was really not an aberration but a mirror image of many other institution's portfolios that were using similar *sophisticated* models to produce an investment strategy. The only saving grace for these other institutional investors was that they had employed less leverage, so they could postpone any forced selling a while longer because of excess collateral. However, a complete liquidation of the LTCM investment portfolio would trigger the value at risk *(VAR)* loss limits of other investors and further exasperate the effects of the liquidity hole as more investors were forced to continue the selling cycle.

LTCM was a casualty of a liquidity hole. LTCM's models failed to account for a change in both liquidity and correlations across the securities in which it had made investments. General market illiquidity risk increased as investor's perceptions of the security specific illiquidity risk in their portfolio was re-evaluated. The result was a spectacular failure.

Financial market history is littered with these failures. Unfortunately, I have little doubt that the future will produce other spectacular busts.

Fascinating Fractals

"When the weather changes, nobody believes the laws of physics have changed. Similarly, I don't believe that when the stock market goes into terrible gyrations its rules have changed."

Benoit Mandelbrot

Benoit Mandelbrot was a mathematician who spent 35 years of his career working at IBM before eventually leaving to become a professor at Yale University.

He coined the term *fractal*. He believed that fractals were useful models of many rough phenomena in the world and in many ways were more natural than the artificially smooth phenomena of traditional measurement. Naturally occurring fractals include the shapes of mountains, coastlines and the structures of plants.

The next time you are holding a head of broccoli take a close look at its structure. The large green heads are arranged in a tree-like fashion on branches that sprout from a stock. If you break a head away from the large stock, what will you see? Green heads arranged in a tree-like fashion on branches that sprout from a stock, but they will be smaller in size than the first head. If you broke another head off of the stock the same pattern would be repeated.

Fractal geometry is the study and measurement of the irregular or roughness in our world. A fractal figure can be divided many times and each time the smaller fractions will look like a replica of the original figure. Broccoli has a fractal pattern because the same roughness repeats itself in every piece.

What Does Broccoli Have to Do With Financial Markets?

Fractals are not only found in nature, but also occur in man-made environments such as architecture, music and financial markets.

In 1961 Mandelbrot began to study the prices of cotton commodity futures. He analyzed the daily, monthly and yearly price changes and found that they did not fol-low the normal bell curve distribution, but instead varied significantly from what was expected. The result was that the standard deviation swung widely and was not a con-stant value.[53]

Mandelbrot proved that, contrary to the foundation of Modern Portfolio Theory, prices do not follow the bell curve and have extreme jumps in price or fat tails (think: standard deviations larger than 5). These fat tails are far more frequent than pre-dicted by a bell curve model of financial markets. As a result, financial markets are much more volatile and uncertain than the current accepted theories of finance would predict.

Patterns That Deceive

Below are eight graphs of financial market price patterns. Some are fakes that were produced by Mandelbrot using fractal geometry and others are produced from actual financial market histories. Which are real and which are the fakes?

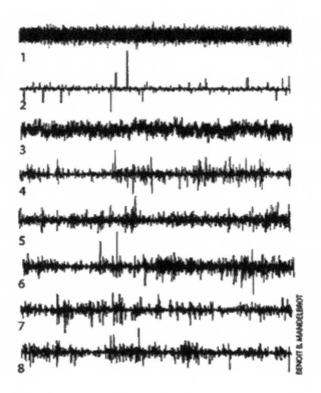

The first graph is extremely repetitive and the price changes are small. Volatility is uniform with no sudden jumps. In a price graph like this, daily prices would vary, but the monthly prices would all be very similar.

The second graph is also repetitive, but it also has a few extreme price jumps. These jumps are isolated events and the overall variability of the price changes remains constant.

The third graph is also repetitive with a pattern of evenly dispersed advances and declines. Although the volatility of the distribution will be greater than in the previous two graphs, there are not any wild price jumps.

The remaining graphs look like various combinations of the first three. They each have repetitive periods that are punctuated by either small or large price changes. Some of the price changes also tend to cluster in groups where periods of price volatility would be extreme.

Did my descriptions help you decide which are the real graphs and which are the fakes?

Chart 1 is a fake and it illustrates the price fluctuations that would be found in a bell curve distribution that is used by Modern Portfolio Theory.

Charts 2 and 3 are also fakes and they were produced in 1963 by Mandelbrot based on what is called a *levy-stable random process.*

Charts 4, 7 and 8 are also fakes created by fractal geometry methods, but at least they look more like actual financial market price histories.

Chart 5 shows the changes in the monthly price of IBM stock from 1959 to 1996 and Chart 6 shows the price fluctuations for the dollar-deutsche mark exchange rate for the same period.[54]

When individual investors are shown these price graphs, very few select the first example as being representative of financial market price behaviour. Investors who have even a small amount of financial market experience understand that price changes are unpredictable and volatile. Modern Portfolio Theory is based on price patterns like those that appear in the first graph, with the result being that the perceived uncertainty in financial markets is being dramatically understated.

Mandelbrot's Rules

Using mathematical models that attempt to measure risk in financial markets is useful only to the degree that it actually reflects the true concern of individual investors about risk (think: How much money can I lose?). Modern Portfolio Theory's use of variance within a bell curve misleads you into accepting an illusion that you can somehow change uncertainty to risk in financial markets and those fat tail losses will be offset by fat tail gains.

Ignoring the reality of fat tail events may be convenient to continue to justify using models that would otherwise be dismissed as unworkable. However, for an individual investor whose investments decline 20% the week before starting retirement, this can be a life altering occurrence.

In Mandelbrot's study of cotton prices he found that, while it was true that price movements were unpredictable, it was not true that they were independent and randomly distributed. In fact, big price moves seemed to bring about other big moves and little moves brought about other little moves. The result was that volatility in the market seemed to *cluster*. Rather than simply ignoring these wild price movements and volatility clusters, he began to develop a theory on why they may happen.

Mandelbrot believed that the randomness of financial markets was not like that produced by flips of a coin, rolls of a dice, or the bell curve model. Instead, the randomness was similar to what occurs based on fractals geometry and the similar patterns that appear in nature. Using a fractal model, price changes do not always eventually revert to the mean and wild individual moves will always occur. More importunately, these wild moves matter and are not just dismissed as rare, one-time events. He theorized that these movements were the result of long-term dependencies that are contained inside the seemingly random movement of market prices.

Mandelbrot created five rules of financial market behaviour:[55]

- *Rule No. 1*: Markets are more uncertain than most individual investors perceive and are much more *risky* than how they are currently measured. Extreme price swings are the norm, not aberrations. Markets behave like oceans and they have turbulence. The turbulence is a complicated phenomenon, with currents, streams, tides and channels that all mingle and affect each other. There is a fractal scaling of turbulence in markets. Some days, prices don't move at all. While on other days, they leap and swoon (think: Leptokurtic distributions). Moreover, there is long-term dependence in the random appearance of markets. For example, if one car company launches a new model that is widely successful and subsequently takes market share from a competitor, there are economic implications for the employees, customers and supplier that can be reflected in equity prices for a long period of time.

- *Rule No. 2*: Market turbulence tends to cluster. Markets are dynamic, unpredictable and sometimes dangerous. Prices do not move slowly and steadily. There is price movement discontinuously, with big jumps in either direction. This discontinuity is one of the main reasons why markets are so much more uncertain than individuals and financial advisors conceive.

- *Rule No. 3*: Prices are not driven solely by events, news and people. A new kind of dynamic surfaces when the participants converge in a marketplace. Different motives, ideas, strategies, tactics, ambitions and needs create an environment that has a life of its own. Fractal analysis provides the mathematical formulas to study patterns that stay the same even though the scale of space or time changes.

- *Rule No. 4*: Markets mislead as they *appear* predictable but are inherent to bubbles and crashes. They deceive because individuals like to see patterns in their world. Due to long-term price dependence, data may show that price changes occur in particular increments or particular directions, but these changes are merely products of chance. Reading meaning into them is pointless. However, prices will scale on a fractal basis with time, so that a chart pattern for a security will have the same movements whether it is for a week, a month, or a decade.

- *Rule No. 5*: In markets, time is relative. Time in financial markets is different than that of the time shown by a clock. Time in financial markets expands and contracts and will not be the same speed for every individual in the market. In periods of high volatility, time seems to speed up while the inverse is true in periods of low volatility.

Mandelbrot viewed himself as a physicist and mathematician rather than a financial market analyst. Although his 2004 work *The (Mis) Behavior of Financial Markets* was viewed as ground breaking in the world of finance, he never completed additional work to expand his fractal view of financial markets. He died in October 2010 at the age of 85.

Scaling and Power Laws

Mandelbrot began a new direction in financial market research that tried to solve the puzzle: if market prices are random, then how can there also be long-term price dependence? The answer may lie in how the internet developed and works.

Physicist Albert-Laszlo Barabási found the existence of a high degree of self-organization that characterized the large scale properties of complex networks.

His study developed a model that mapped the topology of the internet. He discovered connection points, which he called *hubs*. These hubs have many more connections than others parts of the internet and the internet as a whole had a *power-law distribution* of the number of links that are connected to each hub.[56]

A power law is a mathematical relationship between two quantities. When the frequency of an event varies as a power of some attribute of that event (think: the number of links to a web page), the frequency is said to follow a power law. He used the phrase *scale-free network* to describe the class of networks that exhibit a power-law degree distribution.

The power law distribution highly influences the topology of a network, since the major hubs are connected to smaller ones. These are in turn connected to others that are smaller, and so on. Since the vast majority of points in the network only have small connections, a random failure of any point in the network will not likely result in the failure of a major hub. Even if a hub did fail, the network would not lose its connections, because of the links to the remaining hubs. However if a few major hubs randomly failed, the network falls apart. The result is that the hubs are both the strength and a potential weakness of a scale-free network.

Broccoli, the Internet & Financial Markets

Imagine Barabási's scale-free network model of the internet, but replace web pages with "individual investors" and the base for the model is not the internet, but rather "global financial markets".

Individual investors are randomly connected through all the investments they currently have in their portfolios and the decisions they make about their investments. Large financial institutions such as brokerage firms, mutual funds and hedge funds are the largest participants in the marketplace due to the volume of securities they own for themselves and trade on behalf of their clients (think: major hubs). They are also connected to other hubs through derivative contracts, whose value and terms are only known to the other counterparties of the contact. These institutions will also be affected by the orders of the investors who have placed their savings under the management of each hub.

The interaction between individual investors and the large financial hubs is incredibly complex. Each has different motives, ideas, strategies, tactics and ambitions. This complexity in and of itself creates uncertainty. In fact, it makes many of these hubs *too big to fail* because of the connections they have throughout the financial market network.

However, according to Modern Portfolio Theory rational individuals do not interact. They act independently only in their own self-interest and their actions in the market do not affect prices. There are no coordinated signals that should influence other individual investors.

Now think about the reality of the global financial markets. How can a six standard deviation event be possible?

Traders, money managers and individual investors of all shapes and sizes do not act in isolation. They exchange information both formally and informally, and by how their actions in the markets influence prices. This flow of information is continually affecting the financial market network. On most days, the information flows, but the impact on markets is uneventful (think: Mandelbrot Rule No. 4).

Then one day, the exchange of information affects the actions of a hub. This action acts as an influence on all market participants and a crowd of combined actions starts a feedback cycle (think: herding and Mandelbrot Rule No. 3). The impact on markets is significant. Prices jump, volatility increases and clusters (think: Mandelbrot Rule No. 2). Time expands and seems to speed up for all investors and trading in the market takes on a life of its own (think: Mandelbrot Rule No. 3).

All media is now buzzing with market reporting and commentary (think: availability bias). The flow of information and its perceived relevance to all investors increases, but information access is not uniform among investors (think: OTC derivatives and ambiguity aversion). The trading in the market seems to be one-sided and the decisions of all investors become self-organizing (think: Barabási scale free network and herding).

Individual investors sell their holdings and overwhelm the hubs with sell orders. Any semblance of rational decision making is abandoned. Long-term investment goals are forgotten. *Get me out now at any price, before it's too late!!!* (think: automatic brain and changing risk perceptions). Fear, regret and the pain of mounting investment losses now grip individual and institutional investors (think: loss aversion).

A fat tail event has unexpectedly occurred once again and the global financial system seems to be on the brink of failure.

Experience vs. Exposure

Experience is based on the past and considers the probability of future outcomes only in the context of what has previously occurred. *Exposure* considers both the likelihood and the cost of a future outcome that has yet to occur.

Under Modern Portfolio Theory, experience is exposure, until the surprise arrival of the next unpleasant financial market event. It assumes that what volatility has been experienced in the past will be the worst that can be expected in the future. This ignores the fact that all market crashes seem to each set a new precedent for declines.

The chance of a decline as large as 30% or greater should never be ignored, no matter how rare its occurrence is projected to be.

Mathematical formulas based upon the bell curve cannot convert uncertainty into risk, and they do nothing to eliminate the exposure that you have as an investor in financial markets.

CHAPTER 5

THE FINANCIAL ADVICE INDUSTRY: COSTS, CONFLICTS AND CAMOUFLAGE

"He will risk half his fortune in the stock market with less reflection than he devotes to the selection of a medium-priced automobile."

Jessie Livermore, *Reminiscences of a Stock Operator 1932*

What is the Purpose of the Financial Advice Industry?

I have highlighted the plentiful flaws with today's accepted theories of the workings of financial markets that rely on a naïve definition of risk. These flaws revolve around both misinformation and misunderstanding:

- Misinformation is information that, while not necessarily wrong, is misleading (think: focusing on nominal vs. real investment returns).

- Misunderstanding arises through confusion about the real *risk* that is present in financial markets or the principles of probability (think: ignoring the reality that six standard deviation market declines will affect you).

Either of these issues on their own can produce unintended investment consequences. However, when the issues are combined they produce the framework for astonishingly poor investment decisions that overstate long-term rates of return and understate the perceptions of long-term uncertainty.

The financial industry's definition of risk deceives you into believing markets are not uncertain, but merely risky, based on a convenient measuring method that ignores life-altering, fat tail investment events. The heuristic biases you possess further complicate the issue of how you interpret the information you encounter.

Why would the financial advice industry not revise this misinformation in order convey realistic risk and return expectations to clients?

The financial advice industry is motivated by the need to convince you to put your money at *risk*. Simply stated, if they are not successful in this endeavour, they do not get paid.

It is easier to achieve their goal if they understate uncertainty by calling it *risk* and also use heuristic biases to their advantage as part of their investment sales process.

In today's financial marketplace, the investment recommendations of choice are managed money products (think: mutual funds). Now, more than ever before, the primary role of a licensed financial advisor is the sale of investment products disguised as advice.

Financial Advice is Very Big Business

The Canadian Financial Services sector is made up of banks, credit unions, life insurance companies, securities dealers, mutual fund manufacturers and distributors, as well as independent financial advisors.

The financial services sector is a significant contributor to Canada's economic growth, employing over 600,000 Canadians, with a payroll of over $35 billion. The sector represented 6% of Canada's gross domestic product in 2003 and contributed close to $13 billion in taxes to all levels of government. Approximately 90,000 individuals are licensed in various forms to provide financial advice in Canada.[57]

The mutual fund sector consists of both the manufacturers of funds and the distributors, with a number of mutual fund companies involved in both segments of the business. The mutual fund industry has been the fastest-growing segment of the financial services sector since the 1990s. The majority of growth has been due to increased sales.[58]

At the end of 2010, there were 367 mutual fund companies sponsoring over 27,000 funds.[59]

The financial advice industry is governed by provincial securities regulation, which oversees discretionary portfolio managers, investment fund managers and exempt market dealers. There is also industry self-regulation through:

- The Mutual Fund Dealers Association of Canada (MFDA), which oversees the sales distribution of mutual funds.

- The Investment Industry Regulatory Organization of Canada (IIROC), which oversees all investment dealers and trading activity on debt and equity marketplaces.

How Do You Pay For Advice?

There are three basic compensation models for financial advice providers. Although the type of compensation method used should not necessarily be the sole criteria when choosing an advisor, it is important than you understand how you pay for the investment advice you receive.

- **Commission Based**

Commissions can be paid by you directly to your advisor's employer or to the employer by the manufacturer of the investment product after you have made your purchase. These can be a visible payments such as those that occur when you purchase or sell an individual security (think: stock trades); or from a fee that is embedded in the product that was recommended for purchase (think: mutual funds). Many commission payments that are embedded in financial products are not disclosed to you as a specific dollar amount. Embedded payments may also continue for as long as you own the investment (think: mutual funds).

Commission payments are divided between the employer and your advisor, based upon a *compensation grid*. The grid determines how much of the payment goes to the advisor and will vary throughout the year based upon the total amount of commissions produced and the average size of each transaction. This form of compensation is the most common among financial advisors.

- **Salary and Bonuses**

Compensation is paid to your advisor by their employer. You do not remunerate the advisor directly, but you pay for the advice through some type of fee that is embedded in the product that is purchased (think: mutual funds). This is the normal structure you will find for financial advisors who work in a bank branch network. These in-house financial advisors are paid a base salary and bonuses related to the sale of bank products.

- **Asset or Fee Based**

Compensation is paid to your advisor solely by the client and is usually determined by an hourly fee or by a fee that is based on the dollar value of investment assets managed on behalf of the client. The advisor will not receive commissions, finder's fees or other forms of compensation as a result of recommending investments.

The Principal-Agent Problem

When an investment advisor recommends that you purchase a financial product, there can be as many as five participants who have a financial interest in the transaction:

- Yourself as the investor

- Your financial advisor

- The company that employs your financial advisor

- The company that provides the investment management for the product that is purchased

- A lender, if your financial advisor recommends that you borrow to invest.

When the recommended investment is profitable, everyone on this list makes money. However, when the investment experiences a loss, you are the only one of the five participants that suffers. All of the other participants have either been compensated, are still being compensated or have not lost a cent.

The financial advice industry is plagued by a principal-agent problem wherein individual investors (principals) rely on brokers, financial planners and mutual fund sales representatives (agents) for advice. The information asymmetry that is present in this relationship (agents have information that the principals do not) can lead to numerous conflicts of interest.

A conflict of interest is present any time a financial advisor is not thinking exclusively about what is in the best financial interest of the client they are advising. Conflicts can result from an outside influence that affects or biases their judgment.

A commission-based compensation model forms the core of the sales culture that is present in many financial advisory firms. Advisors are required to sell products as part of the process for providing financial advice, since the advisor's pay is linked directly to these transactions. Abuse of this model can occur by:

- Advising you to purchase investment products that are not suitable for your investment needs.

- Generating commissions through the unnecessary buying and selling of securities (commonly known as churning).

- Switching investment assets from one investment product to another so that the advisor can generate a commission.

- Recommending an investment product that pays a higher sales commission rather than a less expensive alternative.

Many individual investors are not aware of the potential conflicts or the abuse that can bias the advice they receive.

Asset-based compensation, providing that it is transparent, can resolve virtually all of the abovementioned conflicts for both advisors and clients. The advisor's compensation is only contingent upon the value of a client's investment assets. As a result, if the advisor is able to increase the asset value, then the advisor's compensation will increase. Conversely, the compensation will decline if the market value of the assets decreases. There is no compensation that is received as a result of transactions or the investment products that are recommended for inclusion in the portfolio.

When an advisor's method and amount of compensation is transparent to you it creates a relationship that is based on shared mutual interests and trust, rather than suspicion regarding whose interests are being served when investment recommendations are provided.

The New Dirty Word

Scrutiny of compensation models as they currently exist in the financial advice industry is increasing; with the result that commission-based models are now being more generally viewed with a jaded eye.

Some financial regulators have introduced new legislation that effectively bans or restricts commission payments to financial advisors. Beginning in 2012, The Financial Services Authority (FSA) in the United Kingdom has banned commissions and will require advisers to charge a fee for providing advice.

The distinction between different types of advice will also be made clearer, with advisers having to describe themselves as either offering "independent advice", or "restricted advice" for recommendations based on a small range of products. The captive sales forces of banks and insurers, who cannot recommend independent products, will be required to disclose the size of their commission payments. All advisers will also be required to hold a qualification equivalent to passing the first year of university.[60]

The Chairman of the FSA stated that the new legislation was required because:

"In many retail financial markets, the imbalances of knowledge and power between consumers and providers are so profound, and the potential for perverse incentives so great, that even highly competitive markets and extensive information disclosure are insufficient to protect consumer interests."[61]

Australia has also introduced new legislation designed to tackle conflicts of interest that "have threatened the quality of financial advice that has been provided to Australian investors". A ban will begin, on July 1, 2012, on commissions and volume-based payments that are related to the distribution and advice of retail investment products. "These reforms will see Australian investors receive financial advice that is in their best interests, rather than being directed to products as a result of incentives or commissions offered to the financial advisor."[62]

Canadian securities regulators are slowly proceeding along a similar path, by implementing a new Fund Facts point-of-sale disclosure document for mutual funds, which would illustrate the costs of buying and owning a fund.

Not surprisingly, the mutual fund industry has responded to the proposal by complaining that requiring delivery of the document before an individual investor makes a purchase is just too cumbersome and costly; and that it is unfair to single out mutual funds for this treatment when other types of investments will not have similar requirements.[63]

In June 2010, the Mutual Fund Dealers Association of Canada proposed a new rule concerning the disclosure of fees and commissions to clients. The purpose of the rule was to improve investor decision making by requiring fund dealers to inform individual investors of transaction fees or charges before accepting an order. In response to the proposal, the industry complained that the new rule was unnecessary and it would be costly to comply with the new requirements.[64]

The resistance by some sectors of the Canadian financial advice industry to efforts aimed at improving cost and compensation disclosure can be viewed as a desire to continue the status quo, which clearly only benefits the industry and the advisors it employs.

Duty and Disclosure

While asset-based compensation does eliminate many potential conflicts of interest that the commission model is based upon, neither model provides any information about the abilities, skills or ethics of an individual financial advisor.

In my opinion, the ongoing debate about compensation misses two key points:

- What is the duty of the advisor to the individual investor receiving the advice?

- Is the compensation that the advisor continues to receive for providing ongoing advice continually disclosed?

Is Your Financial Advisor a Salesman?

A fiduciary is someone who has undertaken to act for and on behalf of another individual in circumstances that give rise to a relationship of trust and confidence.

A fiduciary duty requires a legal and ethical relationship of confidence regarding the management of money between the *fiduciary* and a *principal*. A fiduciary duty is the highest standard of care and requires extreme loyalty to the principal. The word itself originated from the Latin words *fides*, meaning faith, and *fiducia*, meaning trust. In a fiduciary relationship one person is in a position of vulnerability. Therefore, the fiduciary must not put his personal interests before the duty.[65]

Accountants and lawyers often have fiduciary relationships with the individuals they advise. These occupations require a significant investment of time and money to receive the education and professional accreditation required to practice in these fields. Conversely, becoming a mutual fund salesperson is "open to all individuals". There are no academic requirements for entering the Investment Funds Program."[66]

The Investment Funds program requires:

- Completion of the web-based Investment Funds course with a minimum passing mark of 60%. The cost for the course is $375.

- Completion of a training program within 90 days of being registered as a mutual fund salesperson with a provincial securities commission to comply with the Mutual Fund Dealers Association of Canada (MFDA) Rule 1.2.1(c).

So for a few months of study time and $375, a new salesperson is then eligible to be registered with an MFDA firm. Once this has occurred, they are then *qualified* to provide financial advice to you through the sale of mutual funds.

Most individual investors in Canada are unaware that there are different standards of care placed upon financial advisors depending on how they act on behalf of clients. Portfolio managers who act on a discretionary basis when managing investment assets are viewed as having a fiduciary duty to their clients. Financial advisors who make rec-ommendations to clients that require authorization from the client prior to executing the recommendation (think: brokers and mutual fund salespersons), are not held to a fiduciary standard.

Show Me an Invoice

Discretionary portfolio managers invoice their clients directly for their services as they are provided. These fees are disclosed and agreed upon in advance and are billed in a clear, understandable manner.

Financial salespeople are remunerated by commissions that:

- May never be disclosed (think: insurance).

- May only be disclosed if the client does their own investigation prior to acting on the recommendation (think: mutual fund management expense ratios).

- May only be disclosed after a transaction is completed (think: a brokerage trade confirmation).

Why are the commission payments that financial advisors receive from the manu-facturers of the products they recommend so obscure? Would the disclosure of the total dollar amount of these commissions result in an individual investor questioning the value of the *advice* they have received in exchange for the payment? Perhaps the answer lies in the loss of a potential sale.

If financial advisors who are compensated by commissions believe that they should hold themselves out to the investing public as anything other than salespeople, then they should also be accountable under a higher standard of care to their clients. Current reg-ulations may not require this standard of care; however, there is nothing that prevents them from using it as a guiding ethical principal in how they interact with the individual investors they advise.

Rising to this standard can be achieved regardless of the compensation model of the advisor, by providing prospective clients with a disclosure, written in plain language, *prior* to them acting on any advice. The disclosure should describe:

- The total costs, fees and commissions you will pay for acting on the advice received.

- Any potential conflicts of interest that the advisor or the advisor's employer may have with a client.

- How any conflicts will be resolved in the client's favour.

- The services that a client can have access to from the advisor and what services they can expect in return for the disclosed total costs.

If a client continues to pay some type of ongoing annual cost that is embedded in the investment product that they have purchased, then this amount should also be disclosed in writing to the investor at the end of each calendar year.

Written disclosures allow individual investors to understand the total ongoing cost of the advice they are receiving, and if there are any conflicts that may bias the recommendations that are presented to them.

So Is Your Financial Advisor a Salesman?

The answers to the following three questions will provide your answer:

- Did you receive a written disclosure that outlined the total costs and conflicts prior to having any investment recommendations implemented?

- Does your advisor act under a fiduciary standard?

- Do you pay your advisor directly for the ongoing advice you receive, rather than through embedded commissions in the products that are recommended?

The vast majority of the financial advice industry continues to use the camouflage of misinformation and misunderstanding to hide the true amount of uncertainty you accept when you act on their advice. This camouflage is present in many of the sales techniques that are used by the financial advice industry.

Let's remove the camouflage ....

Costs Are Not Equal to Value When You Invest

In today's financial advice industry, managed money and structured products are commonly the investment recommendations of choice from advisors. These products include:

- Principal Protected Notes: that offer equity-like returns and a promise of principal protection.

- Variable Annuities: that offer guaranteed minimum payments over an individual investor's lifetime.

- Wrap Accounts: which combine multi-manager investment management styles and automatic changes to asset allocations.

- Alternative Investments: that offer exposure to non-traditional investment strategies.

- Mutual Funds: which allow individual investors the opportunity to risk their capital in almost every conceivable global financial market or sector.

A common theme that underlies these products is the embedded fees that compensate the investment advice industry in return for their recommendation.

Do individual investors derive value for the fees that they pay?

The Price You Pay

Mutual funds are the most common embedded fee product that is sold to individual investors.

A mutual fund provides a group of investors a structure to pool their capital to make investments. Each investor owns a proportional share of the fund's investments, which are selected by an investment manager according to an overriding investment objective.

You pay a price to participate in a mutual fund. To compensate all parties who were involved in the sale of the product, the mutual fund manufacturer will charge fees to the pool of investment assets. Information regarding the various fees and expenses are outlined in a fund's simplified prospectus. By law this document has to be provided to you as an investor in the fund. In Canada, mutual fund documents can also be found at www.sedar.com.

Mutual Fund manufacturing and distribution is a very profitable enterprise. In fact, Canadian individual investors pay some of the highest mutual fund fees in the world. A study (Khorana, Servaves, Tufano 2007) examined 46,580 mutual funds offered for sale in 18 countries, which accounted for 86% of the entire global mutual fund industry. The study concluded that Canadian investors paid higher fees on their fund investments across all major asset classes.[67]

Out of Sight, Out of Mind

To manage your investment costs, you need to know what they are. However, many mutual fund expenses are not transparently disclosed on your account statement. Some are non-negotiable, while others can be reduced or eliminated at the discretion of your financial advisor.

Typical costs include:

- The Management Expense Ratio (MER): The MER is an annual fee charged directly to the fund's assets to pay for such expenses as:

    - The fee paid to the investment manager

    - The financial adviser's sales commission and ongoing fee, which is usually called a trailer fee

    - Legal and audit fees

    - Custodian and transfer agent fees

    - Administration expenses of the fund

    - GST/HST

The MER is calculated daily as a percentage of a fund's assets.[68]

- Performance bonuses: Some funds pay performance bonuses to their investment managers if they produce a return that exceeds a specified benchmark.

- Front-End loads: Some funds allow a financial advisor to charge an initial sales commission ranging from 1% to 5%. Therefore, you pay your advisor at the time of your initial investment. For example, if you are investing $100,000 in a fund with a 5% load, your advisor is receiving $5,000, and $95,000 is being invested in the fund. However, there are no redemption fees when you sell your fund units.

- Rear-End loads: These fees are also sometimes called deferred sales charges. They occur when you redeem a fund before a specified number of years has elapsed. These fees decline from a high of about 6% in the first year to zero after six years. Under this purchase option you are making a commitment to invest in the fund for six years, otherwise you will pay a penalty. The mutual fund manufacturer provides your advisor with a commission payment (usually 5%), which is eventually recouped by retaining a larger portion of the MER charge.

- Switch fees: Changing your investment from one mutual fund to another fund offered by the same manufacturer can sometimes result in a fee of 1% to 3%. This fee is charged directly to your investment assets.

- Insurance fees: Funds that offer a guarantee to return some portion of your initial investment if you hold the fund for an extended period are often called segregated funds. The cost of this insurance increases the MER compared to a conventional mutual fund.

- Trailer Fees: A mutual fund manufacturer will pay your advisor a fee for as long as you remain invested in a fund. This fee is called a trailer and is designed as a payment to your advisor for any ongoing services they may provide to you. Front-end load funds usually pay an annual 1% trailer, and rear-end load funds pay an annual 0.5% trailer. Trailer fees are included in the fund's MER.

- Trading Costs: A mutual fund incurs trading costs when securities are bought and sold. These costs include brokerage commissions and changes in market prices and are not included in the MER.

The MER Pain Threshold

Do you remember Jerry from Sales Are Us Inc. in Chapter 1? On the advice of his financial advisor, Jerry has decided to invest $250,000 into the Once-In-A-Lifetime Opportunity fund, with the intention of building his savings for retirement over the next ten years.

Jerry is not aware of the amount of the continual MER expense he pays, since it is charged directly to the assets of the mutual fund rather than appearing as a transparent fee on his account statement.

The MER represents the annual rate at which his assets are shrinking, before the fund earns any investment return.

The Once-In-A-Lifetime fund has an MER of 2.50%. Therefore, in the first year of the investment Jerry will pay a fee of 2.50% of his initial investment asset value, leaving 97.5%.

Mathematically the formula is:

$$1 - MER = 1 - 0.025 = 0.975$$

In the second year, Jerry is again charged a fee of 2.50 % on the remaining 97.5%, leaving 95.06%:

$$(1 - MER) \times (1 - MER) = (1 - 0.025) \times (1 - 0.025)$$

The percentage of the investment that Jerry retains can be expressed as:

$$(1 - MER)^n \times 100$$

The MER's rate of erosion on Jerry's investment is independent of the fund's rate of return. The MER continues each and every year, even if the fund has negative investment performance.

Pay As You Go

The fund offers Jerry the ability to invest in different unit classes that will affect the trailer fee his advisor receives for recommending the fund to him.

The Once-In-A-Lifetime Opportunity fund can pay a trailer fee up to 1.00% as part of the 2.50% MER.

There are five different unit classes for the fund and each class will pay a different trailer rate.

- Front-End Load

    This unit class will pay an annual trailer fee of 1.00% of the average value of Jerry's investment for as long as he owns the fund. This fee is in addition to a sales commission of between 0% and 5% that he will pay his advisor when he makes his initial purchase.

- Rear-End Load

    This unit class will pay a trailer fee of 0.25% to 0.50% to Jerry's advisor. The trailer fee is reduced because the advisor will receive a 5% commission of Jerry's initial investment value that is paid by the mutual fund manufacturer.

    The fund manufacturer is reimbursed for this payment by keeping a larger portion of the MER and by any redemption fees that are paid by Jerry if he sells his investment prior to the expiry of the typical six year holding period.

- No Load

    This class does not have initial sales commissions, nor do they have any deferred sales charges. This class of the fund will pay a 1.00% annual trailer fee to Jerry's advisor for as long as he holds the fund.

- Low or Level Load

    This class is similar to a rear-end load class. The initial commission is lower, usually averaging 3%. The redemption fees start at 3% and decline to

0% after three years. However, while the trailer fee begins at 0.25%, it will increase to 1.00% as the redemption fee expires.

- F Class Funds

This unit class does not pay a trailer fee to Jerry's advisor. However, his advisor will charge some form of transparent service or ongoing advisory fee directly to Jerry to compensate him for his ongoing advice.

The total amount of compensation that Jerry's advisor will ultimately receive over his investment time horizon will be very similar under all unit classes, with the exception of the F Class. The only difference is with the timing of when the advisor will be paid.

Since the recommendation you frequently receive from your financial advisor is to hold your investment for the *long-term,* the implied assumption is that you will not have to pay a redemption fee if you purchase rear-end load units. Coincidently, this unit class also has the added benefit of maximizing the initial compensation that your advisor will receive, with a usual embedded commission payment of 5% from the fund manufacturer (think: misinformation).

F Class units allow financial advisors the ability to make the compensation they receive transparent to their clients, rather than receiving payments directly from mutual fund manufacturers. F Class units were first introduced in 2001, however, by December 31th, 2006 they only represented 1.1% of the mutual fund marketplace.[69]

Turnover Lowers Returns

Trading costs have an impact on a mutual fund's investment performance. The level of trading activity in a fund is usually measured by the portfolio turnover ratio (TER).

Canadian mutual funds are required to provide TER information in their semi-annual performance reports to unit holders. The trading cost that is expressed in the TER, is an additional cost borne by fund investors that is not included in the management expense ratio (MER).

A TER ratio of 1 tells you that the value of the entire portfolio was traded in a year (think: 100% turnover of the investments). Funds with high portfolio turnover rates will incur higher trading costs than those that trade less often. The size of the fund's trades also affect trading costs, since brokerage per-share commissions are lower for large volumes compared to smaller volumes. Therefore, trading costs can be a major expense for a small fund that trades frequently.

Although the TER does provide some useful information, it does not capture the entire cost of trading because it ignores the impact of the fund's trading activities on the market prices of securities (think: security specific liquidity risk). Trading results in the fund incurring a cost due to the market price differential that is required to buy or sell securities. This cost will vary among funds and is the result of the fund's own unique investment holdings and decisions.

Research by Kadlec, Edelsen and Evans (2006) examined trading costs of 1,706 U.S. mutual funds from 1995 to 2005. They found that annual trading costs of the funds were *comparable in magnitude* to the management expense ratios (MER). On average, funds failed to fully recover their trading costs. For every $1 spent on trading, assets were reduced by an average of 41 cents. Not only does trading reduce performance; it also predicts lower future returns. The study concluded that the more a fund manager trades, the greater the future performance drag experienced by investors.[70]

This inverse trading-to-performance relationship can largely be attributed to the investment dollars that flow in and out of a fund. The investment capital of a fund is not static and, to some degree, is beyond the control of the investment manager. Managers must buy or sell accordingly to adjust the portfolio for contributions and redemptions. These *flow-driven trades* were shown to be significantly more costly than discretionary trades, which are based only on the manager's decision regarding the investment merits of securities that should be included in the portfolio. Consequently, the actions of each individual investor in a fund can ultimately affect the investment return realized by other investors.

More Trading = More Taxes

Most mutual funds are set up under a legal trust structure and, as such, act as a tax intermediary between you and your proportional ownership in the fund's investment portfolio. As the fund receives interest, dividends, and capital gains or losses from transactions in the portfolio, the tax liability is passed through to you. The allocation of the taxable income is usually calculated just prior to a calendar year end.

Since a mutual fund has many individual investors, the fund cannot maximize the tax efficiency of the portfolio specific to your individual tax circumstances. This has two disadvantages:

- You have no control over the amount of taxable income or transactions that may be allocated to you in a specific year. The ability to defer taxable events to future years is lost. You may have the ability to crystallize a capital gain by selling units of the fund prior to a tax year end, but this type of transaction may result in payment of either a deferred sales charge or a switch fee.

- Since all taxable income and transactions for an entire tax year must be distributed prior to year end, this results in all investors who holds units on the distribution date receiving the tax liability. Therefore, you may be responsible to pay the tax for transactions that occurred in the portfolio prior to the time you were actually a unit holder.

If you must pay the taxes owing on these distributions by liquidating other assets, this may compound your tax liability by requiring you to liquidate other investments, which can result in additional taxes.

Why Investment Costs Matter

Gross investment returns, less costs, equals your net investment return. The value of the costs that you pay represents the transfer of a significant portion of your investment capital to the financial advice industry. However, research confirms that very few individual investors really understand that lower investment cost equals higher returns.

Choi et al (2009) conducted a study using participants from the Wharton and Harvard college campuses. The participants included 391 Harvard staff members, 252 Wharton MBA and Ph.D. students, and 87 students recruited from the general student population. The participants were obviously well educated and were tested to ensure that they possessed greater financial literacy than a typical individual investor.[71]

They were each given a hypothetical $10,000 to invest in any combination of four real S&P 500 index funds. A fact sheet was provided, which explained that all S&P 500 index funds seek to make their before-cost investment returns approximate the S&P

500 Index. Therefore, the only difference in the performance of the funds would be attributable to the amount of management fees they charged investors.

As an incentive to entice participants to carefully consider their investment decisions, they were told that one participant would be selected at random to win any return produced by their chosen investments over a one-year period.

Participants received the prospectuses for each of the four funds, which is usually the document that is sent to potential investors who request information prior to investing. The participants were then divided into groups based upon additional information they would receive prior to making their investment decisions:

- Prospectus-Only Group: received only the prospectuses for each of the funds.

- Effect-of-Fees Group: also received information, which explained that mutual funds charge fees, showed how to calculate the impact of management fees on portfolio values, and listed the expense ratio for a one-year $10,000 investment in each of the four funds.

- Returns Group: also received additional information, which showed the annualized historical returns since the inception of each fund after deducting all fees. The return information also included the disclaimer "past performance is no guarantee of future results."

On average, the participants paid between 112 to 201 basis points more in fees than they needed to when they received only the funds' prospectuses to aid their decision. Staff and the college student participants reported that fees played relatively little role in their investment decisions. The MBAs claimed that fees were the most important decision factor, yet their portfolio fees were not statistically lower than those paid by the other participants. The group who received historical returns placed a large emphasis on this information, despite the fact that the past returns were measured over different time horizons.

Your Silent Partner

"Commissions, trailing commissions, management fees and expenses all may be associated with mutual fund investments. Please read the prospectus before investing. Mutual funds are not guaranteed, their values change frequently and past performance may not be repeated."

This phrase is a required standard disclosure statement that is issued in a mutual fund prospectus and advertisements. Perhaps it should be clearer and instead read:

"The fees and expenses you pay to the financial advice industry are your silent investment partner who will reduce your investment returns"

Most individual investors are unaware of the expenses they incur from their mutual fund investments, because the industry does a very good job of not directly disclosing what you actually pay and when you pay it.

When you are sold an investment product with an embedded fee, you now have a silent partner who participates in the investment with you, and, in many circumstances your own interests conflict with those of your partner.

Investment costs have a significant effect on your investment returns. In fact, the costs you pay will likely have the single greatest impact on the success of your long-term investment performance.

If Jerry's $250,000 investment in the Once-In-A-Lifetime-Opportunity fund produces a pre-tax annual return of 8%, then at the end of his 10-year investment horizon it will be worth $539,731. If he made the same investment, but did not pay the 2.5% MER, then at the end of ten years his investment would be worth $678,520. That is a difference of $138,789 of his investment return that was paid to his financial advisor silent partner.

Over the long-term, the fees you pay for investment products and services will have a significant impact on whether you are successful in achieving your investment goals.

Worth the Price?

Most investments are not bought by individual investors, rather they are sold by financial advisors to individuals who are seeking advice. However, research shows that there is limited evidence of the benefits of professional advice to mutual fund investors.

Do advisors select funds which will provide you with above average future performance?

A Harvard Business School study (2006) found, on a risk-adjusted basis, that mutual funds sold by advisors underperform funds sold through the direct channel (funds sold directly to investors by fund manufacturers). "Clients of advisors, on average, purchase worse performing funds, they pay substantial distribution charges and the recommendations are directed to funds whose distribution fees are richer."[72]

A survey (Jones et al 2005) of 530 financial advisors asked them to rank the importance of 14 mutual fund characteristics that they considered when making recommendations to clients. Not surprisingly, a fund's investment objective was the most important factor, but a fund's expenses ranked eighth. Additionally, advisors placed great emphasis on a fund's past returns by ranking this characteristic equivalent to the investment objective as the most important factor in fund selection. Therefore, financial advisors give high priority to funds that have performed well in the past, despite the evidence that strong past performance does not predict future performance.[73]

Do advisors select funds that require you to pay below average costs?

Similar results were found in a study (Bergstresser et al. 2007) that compared fund choices from 1996 to 2004 by individual fund investors who bought through direct channels, and by those who bought through financial advisors. They found that advisors directed investors toward funds with higher loads. Also, the larger a fund's load, the more investment flow it received from advisor directed investors.[74]

Do advisors overcome heuristic biases to make better investment recommendations?

Financial advisors are also not immune to many of the heuristic biases that affect the investment decisions made by individual investors. There are a number of behavioural studies in the financial planning domain (Roszkowski and Snelbecker 1990) concluding that financial planners are equally susceptible to the framing bias illustrated by Prospect Theory as are individual investors.[75]

Overconfidence bias is also present in the financial advice industry and research shows a significant negative correlation between an advisor's experience and the susceptibility to overconfidence. This implies that many financial advisors do not learn from their past judgment errors and, in fact, become more overconfident over time.[76]

The Myth of Costs

The belief that higher investment costs will produce greater investment performance is a myth. While it's true that, in some circumstances, a higher cost investment may produce a superior investment return, research conclusively shows that this is the exception rather than the rule when measured over long time horizons.[77]

The financial advice industry downplays the importance of costs by repeating the mantra that *fees don't matter, performance matters*. The irony of the *invest for the long-term* philosophy that you frequently receive from your advisor, is that the negative effect of costs on returns becomes more pronounced as the holding period of the investment increases. Your silent partner continues to benefit because their share of your investment return increases as your investment holding period extends.

Investments are available that allow the investment fees you pay to be unbundled and disclosed by financial advisors (think: discretionary managed accounts and F Class units). However, Canada's mutual fund industry caters primarily to the needs of financial advisors rather than individual investors. Fund manufacturers need to compete for product distribution and, as a result, the industry largely resists reducing fees that will affect either their profit margins or the compensation of advisors who sell their products.

The information asymmetry that underlies the principal-agent problem between financial advisors and their clients leads to numerous conflicts of interest (think: sales person vs. fiduciary). Embedded cost structures can create the circumstances whereby some advisors may not always act in their clients' interest, but rather place clients' interests behind their own and those of the mutual fund manufacturers that compensate them.

Investment costs should matter to you because they are the only factor affecting investment performance that you can know with certainty when you make an investment decision. Any money paid for expenses is money that will not be available to compound for your benefit (think: I want to go faster). Understanding and reducing your investing costs should always be a critical factor in your investment decision making process.

Track Records: Fraud, Skill, Chance and Coin Tosses

Mutual fund companies continually tout the returns of funds that have had impressive historical performance as an invitation for investors to join the crowd and participate in the future rewards. It's only common sense that a fund's investment performance must be the result of a superior investment strategy. There could not be other reasons, could there?

Investment success *can and does* result from nothing other than pure chance and, more often than not, investment success is much more likely to result from chance than from genius.

A Million Dollars Delivered to Your Mailbox

We all have our daily routine of reaching inside our mailbox to see what is competing for our attention. It's usually bills, offers to appraise our homes, new approvals for credit cards and advertising flyers. However, today there is also a letter addressed to you from Sounds Convincing Asset Management (SCAM).

The letter from SCAM touts their superior investment skills and informs you that they will prove their prowess by providing you with a series of written monthly investment predictions. The letter contains the first prediction that the S&P/TSX Composite Index will close at a higher level by month end.

You are sceptical because you have heard many predictions from financial firms and advisors that never quite seem to work out as advertised. In fact, your own financial advisor recommended that you invest your retirement assets in a mutual fund that had a stellar record of performance in the previous five years. Unfortunately, that enviable track record seemed to end precisely as you made your investment in the fund.

You toss the letter in the garbage with the other junk mail and forget about it.

One day next month, you reach into your mail box and the SCAM investment logo on the corner of the envelope catches your eye. You think back and recall that the recommendation was about the market moving higher by month end. You open the envelope and sure enough, they confirm that the recommendation they made was accurate and profitable. The letter also asked you to invest with them so that you can profit from their expertise. Thanks, but no thanks you think. Anyone can get lucky once.

The letter contains more detailed information about their investment process and predicts that the market will once again move higher by month end. This letter suffers the same fate as the previous one and ends up in the garbage.

The next monthly letter arrives and highlights another consecutive correct recommendation. It also provides more detail about the history of their star investment strategist and his schooling in Modern Portfolio and the Efficient Market Theories. The letter contains another recommendation, but this time it predicts that the market will decline because of changes in SCAM's view of the economy and the negative effect that will have on stock prices. You have to admit that your interest has increased, but you are still somewhat disbelieving about what is actually occurring with these recommendations.

The letters continue every month for the next year and each prediction proved correct. Each letter contains a reasonable explanation from the SCAM strategists regarding what allows them to make correct investment decisions while other investment advisors fail:

✓   It's our previous experience in financial markets

✓   It's our superior economic forecasting abilities

✓   It's our new models that have identified factors in past financial data that allow us to predict future price changes

✓   We are just simply smarter than those other financial advisors

✓   Etc., etc., etc...

You are now a believer! SCAM has been correct in its monthly prediction fifteen times in a row! That is a track record that cannot be produced by luck alone. Besides their description of how they choose investments makes sense, since you hear other financial gurus saying similar things on CNBC. Even your own financial advisor has mentioned some of these factors in your past meetings. Speaking of your financial advisor, what has this guy done for me lately? The mutual fund he recommended is still not performing the way he predicted and it doesn't have a track record anywhere close to what you could have made if you simply followed the advice of SCAM.

SCAM's letters have always offered to take over the management of your portfolio and now you think that its time you gave them a call. SCAM points out that if you had invested only $10,000 fifteen short months ago and followed their recommendations, you would now have over a $1,000,000. Your time to retirement is quickly approaching and you want to get your investment assets in the control of a financial advisor who actually will make you some money.

Now think to yourself, how could SCAM make an accurate prediction fifteen consecutive times? There must be a trick, but how can it be done if the prediction is given in advance about the direction of the S&P /TSX Composite Index? This is not some small fly-by-night junior mining company that can be controlled by a sneaky promoter; this is an index that is based on the share prices of the largest companies in Canada.

SCAM's investment process is ingenious, convincing and also a fraud. Anyone can produce this series of incredibly *accurate* predictions about the future direction of the market. All that is needed is a list of 131,072 mailing addresses.

The investment *recommendations* work like this:

1. Scam starts with a list of 131,072 individual mailing addresses and then divides the list into two groups.

2. One group is sent a letter with the prediction that the S&P/TSX Composite Index will rise and the other group receives a letter predicting it will decline.

3. At the end of the month, the names in the group that received the wrong prediction are removed from the mailing list.

4. The process repeats, until at the end of 15 months there are 4 individuals who believe that SCAM can make investment recommendations that would have turned their $10,000 into $1,000,000.

Are All Incredible Investment Track Records Frauds?

Of course not, but they may also not be the result of ingenious investment strategies either.

Bill Miller is known for his track record as the manager of the Legg Mason U.S. Value Fund. He initially co-managed the fund from its inception in 1982 and then took sole investment management responsibility in 1990, the year before the track record began to shine. For 15 straight years beginning in 1991 and ending in 2006, the fund had annual returns that were higher than those of the S&P 500 Index. It produced an average annual rate of return of 15.8% for investors in the fund for that 15-year period of time, compared with 11.9% for the S&P 500 Index.

Miller's stock selection philosophy defied conventional investment wisdom. Miller believed that a stock's investment merit should be evaluated by the worth of the underlying business, rather than by comparing the stock's current market price to its future projected earnings.

He calculated a company's business value based on how revenues were produced, and then valued each piece separately. The values of each piece of the business were then measured against a peer industry. The final step was to combine the values together and then divide the total by the outstanding shares to determine the company's worth per share. This number was then compared to the current market price to determine which investments had merit.[78]

Miller believed that his investment team has the edge with its high information diversity of different skill sets among the eight portfolio managers. Miller attributes his success as a money manager to intellectual rigour. "One of the important drivers to the process is that I don't have an MBA," he says. "I bring a tool kit from philosophy, which involves careful logic and precise argumentation to not rule things out in advance."[79]

The record of investment performance brought him fame in the U.S. mutual fund industry. He was selected as "Fund Manager of the Decade" in a poll of Morningstar. com equity analysts in 2000.

In December 2005, Legg Mason completed an asset swap with Citigroup that gave it control of Citigroup's $400 billion investment division, to allow a much larger sales force to market Legg Mason's mutual funds to a much broader pool of customers.

As Miller's track record extended it became the focus of increased marketing publicity, the assets in the fund grew from $750 million in 1990 to over $12.1 billion in

February 2006. Many analysts and investors believed that the track record justified owning the fund despite an expense ratio of 1.68%, that was higher than the 1.5% average for comparable funds.[80]

The fund also charged an additional 0.95% fee to cover the commissions paid to financial advisors who recommended the fund, and to cover advertising costs. Based upon the February 2006 asset value, the total annual fee paid by fund investors to Legg Mason was $318,230,000.

Skill or Luck?

Was Bill Miller's track record luck, skill or some combination of both?

If you select a fund manager *at the start of a specific year* and then calculate the odds that by pure chance the manager you selected would outperform the market in each of the next 15 years, then the odds would be exceptionally low. It is the same odds as flipping your coin and watching it come up heads 15 times in a row (1 in 32,768).

But what if a thousand fund managers are tossing coins once a year and they have been doing so for decades? What are the chances that one of them will toss heads for 15 consecutive years? These odds are much better than those of one pre-selected manager tossing 15 heads in a row.

If you start with a sufficiently large sample of money managers, the probabilities increase that one of them will have such a streak of performance (think: sample size matters). If there is a constant percentage of fund managers that will outperform the market each year (say 50%), you can calculate the probability that one manager will outperform each and every year.

If 1000 fund managers start an annual coin tossing tournament, after the 1st year ½ will toss heads. After the second year ¼ of the managers will have tossed heads, after the 3rd year 1/8th will have tossed heads.

Probability That One Fund Will Outperform Each Year

# of Years		Percentage of Funds that Outperform the Market			
		30%	40%	50%	60%
1	1 in	3	3	2	2
2	1 in	11	6	4	3
3	1 in	37	16	8	5
4	1 in	123	39	16	8
5	1 in	412	98	32	13
6	1 in	1,372	244	64	21
7	1 in	4,572	610	128	36
8	1 in	15,242	1,526	256	60
9	1 in	50,805	3,815	512	99
10	1 in	169,351	9,537	1,024	165
11	1 in	564,503	23,842	2,048	276
12	1 in	1,881,676	59,605	4,096	459
13	1 in	6,272,255	149,012	8,192	766
14	1 in	20,907,516	372,529	16,384	1,276
15	1 in	69,691,719	931,323	32,768	2,127

After 15 tosses, the chances that a particular coin tosser that you identified at the beginning of the contest will have flipped all heads are 1 in 32,768. However, the chance that *anyone* among the original 1000 fund managers will have tossed all heads is about 3%.[81]

While the coin tossing contest illustrates that the odds are not extreme that some investment manager can produce a seemingly impressive track record merely by chance, there are also a number of critical issues that are conveniently ignored in the marketing of Bill Miller's track record.

While it is true that the annualized return of his fund exceeded the return of the S&P 500 index for 15-year period:

- For an individual investor to receive the average annual rate of return of 15.8% compared to 11.9% for the S&P 500 Index, they had to be invested at the start of the period and reinvest all dividends that the fund distributed into additional fund units for the entire 15 years. Any individual who purchased the fund at a different date would have received a different rate of return. If only the three best years of the performance history are removed, the fund's annualized results would be only slightly better than those of the S&P 500. Therefore, an individual investor's entry point mattered greatly in what return they received, despite the 15-year track record.

- Miller produced annual returns that were better than the S&P 500 Index, when measured on a relative basis. This does not imply that the fund's returns were positive each year. In fact, there were several years during the track record period when the fund had negative double digit returns, but these were better than those produced by the S&P 500 Index. If you were an investor in the fund, the value of your investment would have lost money during those negative return years.

- The focus on a period of annual returns that begins January 1st and ends on December 31st is a key contributing factor to the longevity of the performance history. There is no theoretical reason why one calendar year is an appropriate holding period, even though it is widely used to measure performance. If rolling 12-month time frames were used over the 15 years, Morningstar calculated that there were 19 periods where the fund underperformed the S&P 500 index.[82]

- The track record was not based on risk-adjusted returns, where the volatility of the fund return is measured against that of the S&P 500 Index benchmark. In fact, the volatility of Miller's fund was much greater than the S&P 500 Index to which it was being compared. Therefore, individual investors in his fund for the 15-year performance history did get a higher rate of return, but they also experienced much more volatility than would have been produced by an investment in the S&P 500 index.

- The track record that was marketed to individual investors started in 1991 and ended in 2006, but Bill Miller was involved as a money manager of the fund since its inception in 1982. Why was the track record from the inception of his investment management responsibility not relevant, because this is actually when he started *flipping his coin*? It's ignored because it would mean that the performance record of the fund would have been nothing exceptional.

When the streak ended, it really ended. Miller underperformed the market for five consecutive years. Investors that made investments in the fund as far back as 1997, barely broke even and, in many cases, suffered significant losses. In 2008 alone, the fund declined 55.1%! The performance collapse wiped out the fund's record streak and resulted in the fund's historic performance comparing poorly when measured against similar funds.

The fund's assets under management have now fallen from $16.5 billion to $4.3 billion, reducing Legg Mason's fees with them. Since a large portion of the investment capital that investors placed in the fund arrived near the end of the streak, most of the investors will have received less than the expected returns based upon the perception that the streak would continue into the future.

The US Value Trust Fund used selective math and great marketing to reap large fees, while individual investors were left with dashed investment expectations.

Was it Skill or Luck?

Stock prices are random sequences intertwined with underlying patterns of long-term dependence (think: Mandelbrot Rule #4). Any individual investor or mutual fund manager who is trying to outperform a market index by selecting some securities and excluding others, believes that they have some special ability that allows them to perform better than a random sequence.

When you view the outcome of a random process, it is easy to detect patterns that you believe have meaning, but they are really a simple way to delude yourself into believing you have control over random outcomes (think: illusion of control). Elements of luck or skill may allow outperformance to occur for some period, but eventually randomness overcomes the fortunes of all investment soothsayers.

Bill Miller was likely the *chosen flipper* based on the 3% odds that I outlined in the investment manager coin flipping tournament, but he was also assisted by how the streak was measured and marketed.

The more troubling question is:

Why are investment performance streaks sold to individual investors, when the investment advice industry knows that they are an illusion?

Past Performance Is Not a Guarantee of Future Returns

Regulatory requirements for all communications that show mutual fund performance must contain a disclosure that is similar to this:

"Past performance is not a guarantee of future returns"

If this statement is accurate (and it is), then why do mutual funds advertise and financial advisors sell investments to individual investors like it is not true?

When was the last time that you saw an advertisement for a mutual fund that didn't include some gaudy series of positive past performance numbers?

Has your financial advisor ever recommended that you purchase a mutual fund while also showing you consecutive negative annual returns as the basis for his recommendation?

When you are presented with a new potential investment opportunity, your brain will link the potential investment to the potential future reward. For many types of investments, these potential future rewards cannot be known with certainty. Therefore, you, or your financial advisor, try to remove this uncertainty by looking to the past to confirm your decision (think: availability bias and ambiguity aversion). The result is that you avoid investments that have poor performance histories and instead favour those that have done well.

Individual investors and financial advisors do not heed these past performance disclosure warnings, because they seem to defy common sense. Superior fund managers should always have a good track record compared to poor fund managers, right? If not, how does my financial advisor know where to invest my assets?

In fact, past performance is nearly worthless as a predictor of future results. A study of mutual fund performance (Cathart 1997) evaluated 1,892 diversified U.S. equity funds from 1962 to 1993 and found that:

"Funds in the top decile differ substantially each year, with more than 80% annual turnover in composition. In addition, last year's winners frequently become next year's losers and vice versa. While the ranks of a few of the top, and many of the bottom, funds persist, the year-to-year rankings on most funds appear largely random"[83]

Why would the past performance of a mutual fund's returns not persist?

- It can be a result of pure chance rather than skill (think: the investment manager coin flipping tournament).

- It can be the result of particular investment themes moving in and out of favour. For example, equities in the commodity or technology sectors tend to perform as groups and provide large, short-term returns. Therefore, when a particular fund manager's style is in vogue, the fund will post strong returns only to disappear when the investment environment changes.

- Newly created or small funds can sometimes post good short-term performance records, because they have the ability to invest in a small number of concentrated investments. For a fund with a small amount of investment assets under management, a few successful initial investments will have a large impact on performance. However, as the fund's assets under management grow larger and the investment holdings expand, it becomes more difficult to sustain the initial results.

Like Dogs Chasing Cars

The belief among individual investors and financial advisors that chasing past returns is a productive endeavour is further reinforced by mutual fund rating companies. A large component of this type of ranking methodology relies on past performance as a key characteristic.

Morningstar is widely viewed as having the most influential rating system in the mutual fund industry. Russell Kimmel, the director of mutual fund research at Morningstar, published an article (2002) on Morningstar.com to discuss the rating system Morningstar used to rate mutual funds.

The rating system is a quantitative measure that's updated monthly. Mutual funds are graded on a curve, with 10% of funds getting one star, 22.5% getting two stars, 35% getting three stars, 22.5% getting four stars, and 10% getting five stars.

The star rating is designed to provide a quick summary of a fund's *past* risk-adjusted performance. According to Mr. Kimmel:

"We recognize that what most investors care about, is whether it can predict future performance."[84]

A study by The Federal Reserve Bank of Atlanta (2001) investigated the influence of the Morningstar rating system on individual investor decision making by estimating the value of a *star* in terms of the asset flow it generates for the typical fund. The study found that an initial five-star rating results in average six-month abnormal flow of $26 million, or 53% above normal expected flow. The authors believed this to be evidence that some investors vigilantly monitor this information and view the rating change as *new* information on fund quality. The authors concluded that "Morningstar ratings have unique power to affect asset flow." [85]

Make Hay While the Sun Shines

Advertising benefits mutual fund companies by increasing the flow of new investment dollars into the advertised fund. Unfortunately, these advertisements do not help individual investors make better investment decisions. Instead, they exploit the tendency of individuals to chase past returns (think: availability bias).

Advertising is intended to persuade an audience to purchase products. Ads have two central features that make them an unlikely source of relevant information for individual investors:

- They rarely contain new information.

- They will never portray a product or a company in an objective manner.

Mutual fund ads use marketing techniques that are known to increase the likelihood that the advertisements are noticed (think: size and colour) and be read (think: text length and celebrity endorsements). The advertisements are not designed to provide information that is necessary for optimal investment decisions.

Mutual fund advertising works, since many individual investors are unable to distinguish true information from biased opinions, so they react to advertising.

A study by Jain and Wu (2000) found that mutual funds that advertised in Barron's or Money magazine experienced approximately 20% greater inflows than similar funds that did not advertise. The more heavily the funds advertised, the greater the amount of new investment funds that they received.[86]

Fund companies know that individual investors and advisors chase past returns, so they strike when the "iron is hot" and advertise when past performance is likely to be viewed favourably. In another study of mutual fund advertising (Mullainathan and Shleifer 2005) past returns were mentioned in 62% of fund ads in Money magazine and in 59% of equity fund ads in Business Week.[87]

Mutual fund companies also advertise the Morningstar five-star rating that is awarded to their funds, which acts to further reinforce the value of these ratings with individual investors and advisors. A Federal Reserve Bank of Atlanta study (2001) found that, of thirty-three funds that advertised a Morningstar Rating, eighteen, or 55%, had a 5-star rating and 45% had a 4-star rating. No funds advertised less than a 4-star rating.[88]

Although advertising benefits fund companies, little evidence exists that it also benefits individual investors. In fact, after being advertised, the performance of funds tends to underperform a benchmark that they exceeded before being advertised.[89]

Any advice you receive, or advertising you read, that implies a mutual fund *will do* well in the future because it *has done* well in the past, is taking advantage of your heuristic biases (think: representativeness). The mutual fund industry perpetuates the hot hand myth so that they have something to sell you.

Financial advisors want you to believe that they hold the key to your investment success. In the vast universe of mutual funds (think: 27,000 funds in Canada) advisors will always be able to find some fund that has an impressive track record based on its previous history. This is the fund that will be sold to you. Unfortunately, the likelihood that you will continue to benefit from this performance well into the future is stacked heavily against you.

What is *Good* Investment Performance?

Three years after Jerry made his investment in the Once-In-A-Lifetime Opportunity fund, he had received a 3% annual rate of return. His financial advisor explained to him that, because of the volatility that the markets experienced, he should consider this to be *good* performance. Jerry understood that there were some large price swings in the market, but he also read in the investment section of the weekend newspaper that the S&P/TSX Composite Index had increased 7% over the same period.

Why was the return produced by the Once-In-A-Lifetime Opportunity fund good, rather than bad or average?

Investment returns are difficult to assess in isolation. To meaningfully evaluate the performance of your investments, the results need to be placed in a relevant comparative context. Therefore, the appropriate way to measure performance is by comparing the return you receive with a *benchmark*.

An effective benchmark must exhibit the following properties:

- It should be available to you as a direct investment.

- It should have similar risk and style properties as your investment (think: apples to apples comparison).

- It should be easy to measure.

- It should be specified at the time your original investment was made.

Since a numerical absolute return (think: a real return of 5% annually) is not available as a direct investment, it does not make a valid benchmark. However, it can be used as an investment objective to further enhance the evaluation of your investment performance.

So what can be used as a benchmark?

Broad financial market indexes, for example the S&P/TSX Composite Index, meet the criteria for benchmarks.

The Myth of Active Management

The Once-In-A-Lifetime Opportunity fund is typical of the vast majority of mutual funds that are sold to individual investors by financial advisors. The investment manager of the fund will perform some type of analysis that will result in the purchase of certain securities that are projected to be attractive investments. As new information becomes available and market prices of the securities change, the holdings in the fund's portfolio will be *actively* revised.

The core principle that underlies active investing is that it is possible to identify inefficiencies in the prices of securities that can then be exploited. For this to be true, the profit realized must exceed the cost of researching and transacting in the chosen securities and also surpass any unexpected losses that may occur.

Active investment management can only make sense under two conditions:

- You believe that it is possible to achieve superior returns compared to a benchmark financial market index *after all costs;*

AND

- You can identify those managers who can achieve this superior performance *before* it occurs.

There is an overwhelming amount of academic research showing that the average individual or investment manager, who uses an active approach to portfolio management, will fail to outperform a benchmark index.

How could this be?

I have identified numerous biases with the investment decision making of individual investors (think: heuristic biases) and flaws in the theories that underpin Modern Portfolio Theory and market efficiency (think: foundation cracks). Can no one make a profit by overcoming these obstacles?

The futility of active management as a whole is simple math. This was explained by Nobel laureate William Sharpe:

"Properly measured, the average actively managed dollar must underperform the average passively managed dollar, net of costs. Empirical analyses that appear to refute this principle are guilty of improper measurement."[90]

The key phrase is "average actively managed dollar". There is no question that in some circumstances and time periods an actively managed mutual fund can beat a market index (think: Bill Miller). Every year many of them do, but as the time horizon increases, the number of funds that can maintain their outperformance decreases.

The returns received by all investors in a financial market are zero-sum (think: the sum of the gains must equal the sum of the losses), since all securities are held by someone. Therefore, if some investors receive above average returns, other investors have to receive below average returns. Not all investors can receive above average returns all the time.

The extra costs required to perform active management (think: research, trading and sales commissions) mean that even an investor who receives a superior pre-cost return will continually have this return eroded by these costs.

Any outperformance can only be identified in hindsight (think: dogs chasing cars). Costs and the zero-sum random nature of security price changes (think: Mandelbrot Rule #1) will ensure that any previous outperformance is not likely to persist uninterrupted into the future. Therefore, trying to select a strategy or investment manager that will provide consistent outperformance of a benchmark index is just a version of the shell game that all individual investors will eventually lose.

Mercy Killing

Survivorship refers to how the mutual fund industry makes the historical results of underperforming mutual funds *disappear* through mergers and liquidations. As a result, the overall performance histories of funds that are currently available for sale from a fund manufacturer appear better than they should, because the poor performers and their unappealing track records are no longer visible.

There is a strong relationship between MER costs and survivorship, which compounds the negative attributes of high cost funds.

A study (Carhart et al 2001) tracked the effects of survivorship across the U.S. mutual fund industry from 1962 to 1995. 2071 funds were being marketed when the study began, but only 1346 survived until the study's completion. 725 funds *disappeared;* with an annual average attrition rate of 3.6% (2.2% vanishing due to merger and 1.0% being liquidated). Not surprisingly, disappearing funds produced considerably poorer performance than the surviving funds and most funds disappeared after periods of poor multi-year performance.[91]

There are independent companies that evaluate the performance of mutual funds offered for sale in Canada compared to appropriate financial market index benchmarks. Included in these comparisons are adjustments to account for funds that may have merged or been liquidated during the period under study.

Analysis by Standard & Poors over a 5-year period ending December 31st, 2009 showed that *only* 7.4% of actively managed funds in the Canadian Equity category have outperformed the S&P/TSX Composite Index. Therefore, 92.6% of the individual investors who were sold an actively managed Canadian equity fund would have received superior investment performance, before transactions costs, from an investment in the S&P/TSX Composite Index. The majority of funds produced a performance shortfall that was larger than the differential that could be attributed solely to the MER.[92]

Unfortunately, there is nothing unique above this 5-year period that skewed Canadian equity mutual fund performance lower. These studies consistently show the number of funds that outperform the benchmark over rolling 5-year time horizons to be only in the range of 1-5%. This underperformance is also present across the spectrum of mutual fund investment categories.

During the same study period, only 46.8% of Canadian equity funds survived for the entire period, which means that 53.2% of the funds that were in existence five years ago were either merged or liquidated.

This continual merging and liquidation of poorly performing funds provides an inflated perception of previous fund returns, since many databases that are available to individual investors make no adjustments for survivorship.

Conflicts? What Conflicts?

Jerry receives a letter in the mail from the manufacturer of the Once-In-A-Lifetime Opportunities fund announcing that the fund will be merging with the Exceptional-Second-Chance fund.

Jerry calls his financial advisor to ask about the merger and he learns that the merger is occurring because of the disappointing performance of the fund. The Once-In-A Lifetime fund's past performance was 3%, while the Exceptional-Second-Chance fund's performance was 5% over the same period. The advisor also tells Jerry that financial market conditions have now changed, so his projection is that the strategy of the Exceptional-Second-Chance Fund is now more likely to be successful as long as Jerry is patient and stays invested for the long-term. Jerry asks the advisor about the costs associated with the new fund and he is told that the MER is 2.75%. This is higher than the original fund, but the costs are worth it since the past performance is better.

Jerry wonders why, if the original strategy was not successful, would the fund manufacturer not just liquidate the fund and return his money to him?

The compensation paid by mutual fund investors to financial advisors and fund manufacturers (think: 80% of the MER) is based primarily upon asset gathering and retention, rather than performance.

Mutual fund manufacturers want to maximize assets under management (think: their market share) and the resulting management fees that are calculated on the value of these assets. Therefore, the merger of underperforming funds is much more appealing than liquidation.

The often repeated philosophy of *buy and hold for the long-term* also plays directly into this compensation model because, once individual investors have purchased a fund, they will generally hold it until they are advised to sell. Rear-end load mutual funds with deferred redemption charges represent a *gotcha* moment by the financial advice industry, since this structure essentially locks you into paying six years of MERs, or a redemption penalty if you sell early. These fees are charged whether or not the future performance meets your expectations, or the original projection that was provided to you by your financial advisor.

Buy, Hold & Prosper?

The financial advice industry is built upon the entrenched naive premise of active investment management. Consistent evidence that proves the futility of active manage-ment is largely ignored and the vast majority of investments sold by financial advisors continue to be based upon these strategies.

There are investments that replicate the performance of financial market indexes and outperform an overwhelming majority of actively managed mutual funds, which charge MERs that are only a fraction of that charged by many actively managed funds. The last chapter of this book will have a more detailed discussion of these types of investments.

With 80% of a MER being paid as compensation, why would the financial advice industry take a pay reduction to provide you with superior investment performance?

The Mathematics of Losses

Five years ago John was meeting with his bank manager to renew his mortgage, when the manager asked how his investment portfolio was performing.

John thanked him for being concerned about his welfare and then realized that his question may have not been that altruistic. John remembered that most of the major banks have their own investment brokerage divisions and some branch staff have licences to sell mutual funds.

John told the bank manager that his portfolio hadn't really lived up to his expecta-tions based on what his existing advisor had projected two years ago when he became his client. The market had crashed a year ago and no one seemed to see that coming. His advisor told him that it was one of those rare once in a lifetime events and to be patient, because he expected that the market value of his portfolio would eventually come back. John was still nervous though, because his retirement date was now only five years away. He didn't have a company pension plan because he had transferred these assets to an RRSP account. His financial advisor assured him that the investments he would select in his RRSP should provide him with a better rate of return than what he could expect from his Federal government-sponsored, indexed pension plan. John's savings were now his largest asset and would determine what kind of lifestyle he would enjoy in retirement.

The bank manager then offered to have one of his staff provide John with a second opinion on his portfolio. It was a free service, so John couldn't see the harm in having a discussion.

John met with the designated branch financial planner. She looked young, but assured him that her previous two years working in the bank's commercial lending division, and her rigorous three month mutual fund sales training program gave her enough expertise that he could confidently turn the investment responsibility for his savings over to her guidance.

John completed a six question form to evaluate his risk tolerance and informed her that he had five years before he planned to retire. She entered this information into her investment advisory computer program. A key finding of the analysis was that, since his portfolio value was now less than when he started investing two years ago, and he only had five years until beginning retirement, John would need to obtain a higher rate of return to meet his investment goals. Therefore, John needed to increase the amount of *risk* he was willing to take with his investments to get a higher rate of return. The financial planner presented John with a glossy report that had several graphs showing projections of how his portfolio could grow in the future based upon the impressive track records of several of the bank's mutual funds.

John thought about the recommendation and reviewed the mutual funds that were shown in the report. Their track records over the past two years looked much better than the funds in which he was currently invested, so he decided to switch his investments into what was recommended by the bank financial planner. After all, he hadn't heard from his current financial advisor for over a year.

The bank financial planner completed the transfer forms, which required him to sell all his existing fund investments so that he could buy the newly recommended funds. John didn't realize that he had to pay a 1% deferred sales charge when he sold his current investments, but he thought that it was worth it, since the new investments would certainly do better than his previous holdings.

For the next two years, John felt better about his investment portfolio. The returns of his new funds were decent, but a little less than what he expected based upon the track record he had been shown. It turned out that the old funds that were recommended by his previous advisor had actually improved their performance since he sold them. In fact, they were now actually performing better than his new investments, but at least he was making money so that made him feel better about his decision to change his investments.

When the market decline happened, it seemed to come out of the blue. Everything that he had read in the newspaper and seen on television, only days before, contained projections about how the economy and financial markets could keep moving higher for years. Even the quarterly report he received as part of his mutual fund statement said that there was nothing but clear sailing ahead. Who knew that a series of losses on derivatives by a small Spanish bank he had never heard of could cause a 30% drop in his portfolio value in one week?

John called his bank financial planner to get her opinion on what to do, but she had moved back into a commercial banking job a month ago. He spoke with the new planner that had been assigned to his account.

He laid out his current investment situation to his new advisor. He had just lost 30% of the market value of his account and he only had three years left to retirement.

The new advisor said not to worry, be patient and the market will eventually recover by 30% so that his portfolio's market value would then be the same as it was before the market decline. John thought that, if he could just get the value of his account back to its previous peak, then his retirement would be fine.

John felt much better after the conversation, because what his planner said seemed to make sense. If the market could decline by 30%, then it could also *rise* by 30% and that would allow him to get his money back. John wouldn't make any additional return in his account, but at least he would get back to the same portfolio value he had before the latest decline. Even if a full recovery didn't happen by the time he needed to start using the portfolio to fund his retirement, it shouldn't make that much of a difference. After all, all his financial advisors have told him that market prices always eventually recover; he just needs to be patient.

Now it is time to test your math skills. Will a 30% advance after a 30% decline get John's portfolio back to the same market value?

The answer is no. It will actually take a gain of 42.9% to allow John to recover his lost capital. How can that be?

$500,000 starting portfolio value
A 30% loss equals ($150,000)
$350,000 ending portfolio value

$350,000 portfolio starting value
30% gain equals $105,000
$455,000 ending portfolio value

$350,000 portfolio starting value
42.9% gain equals $150,000
$500,000 ending portfolio value

The mathematics of gains and losses is illusive to many individual investors. A 50% gain does not allow a portfolio to recover from a 50% loss. In fact, a 100% gain is required to restore a 50% loss.

The mathematical relationship between losses and gains can be expressed as:

% gain required to restore loss = [1 / (1 - % Loss)] - 1

The gain required to restore John's 30% is:

[1 / (1 - .30)] - 1 = .429 or 42.9%

As an investment loss increases in size, the gain that is required to restore the loss begins to increase at a faster rate. This is called a nonlinear relationship.

What happens if a gain comes before a loss?

$500,000 portfolio starting value
30% gain equals $150,000
$650,000 portfolio ending value

$650,000 portfolio starting value

30% loss equals ($195,000)

$455,000 portfolio ending value

$$[1 / (1 - .30)] - 1 = .429 \text{ or } 42.9\%$$

John still needs a 42.9% return to allow his portfolio to recover to its previous value of $650,000. Therefore, the order of the gains and losses does not change the nonlinear relationship.

The table below illustrates the recovery rates that are required for losses:

Loss	Required Recovery
10%	11.1%
20%	25.0%
30%	42.9%
40%	66.7%
50%	100%
60%	150%
70%	233%
80%	400%

Father Time Is a Stern Disciplinarian

Individual investors have two distinct time horizons that occur over their investment lives:

- An accumulation phase: where the focus is on saving.

- A withdrawal phase: where the focus is on spending.

You have a finite time horizon to build wealth that is determined by your own mortality. Even if you are a diligent saver, you will likely only have 40 years as an accumulation phase before retiring from the workforce and starting some type of a withdrawal phase.

Traditional measures of risk only focus on the size of investment losses (think: bell curve and standard deviation). These measures of risk make no mention of either:

- The length of time over which a loss is experienced.

- The length of time that is required to recover from the loss.

If you have a 40-year window to build wealth and suffer a large loss that will require multiple years to recover, the loss impairs your ability to build wealth.

What happens if you experience a 30% portfolio loss and are then only able to produce 7% annual returns?

You would need six years of 7% annual gains to recover the loss, but those six years also represent 15% of your total wealth building years. Those six years have been removed from your accumulation phase and will never return.

John lost 30% of the market value of his portfolio and only had three years left until the start of his retirement. He now requires a gain of 42.9% to allow his portfolio value to recover to its previous peak valuation. However, there was no mention of the time that may be required to allow this recovery to occur. It could be six months or five years.

He believed that the recovery time didn't really matter, because he was willing to be patient. Even if a full recovery didn't happen when he needed to start using his portfolio to begin funding his retirement, it shouldn't make that much of a difference.

Recovery times for losses matter greatly. In fact, they matter even more when an accumulation phase is ending and a transition to a withdrawal phase is beginning.

Withdrawal & Recovery

The mathematical implications of a recovery from a loss are more dire for an individual investor that has begun a withdrawal phase. This is due to the fact that the required return must exceed the withdrawal rate in order to begin contributing toward recovering the lost capital value.

A 30% portfolio loss required a gain of 42.9% to recover the value. The time required to produce the 42.9% could be one year, or it could be several.

The table below shows that the larger the subsequent rate of return following the loss, the shorter the time period required to recover the loss.

Loss	1 Year	2 Years	3 Years	4 Years	5 Years
30%	42.9%	19.5%	12.6%	9.3%	7.4%

Using John's example of three years until retirement would require his portfolio to receive an annual compound rate of return of 12.6% to recover his lost capital.

What happens if the recovery rate of return falls short or alternatively, what would happen if John's withdrawal phase began immediately after the 30% market decline occurred?

If the required beginning annual withdrawal rate from the account is 5% and to cover the effects of inflation, this rate will also need to increase annually by 3% (think: real rate of return).

The 30% portfolio loss now requires a gain of 61.8% to recover the lost value and cover the required withdrawals. The time required to produce the 61.8% can be one year or it could be several.

Loss	1 Year	2 Years	3 Years	4 Years	5 Years
30%	61.8%	31.3%	22.6%	18.5%	16.2%

If the portfolio fails to generate these required annual rates of return, then the capital value of the portfolio will erode further.

In 2008 the S&P 500 Index declined 37%. What do you think the financial future holds for individual investors who begin their retirement in January 2009?

Drawdowns vs. Losses

A drawdown measures the *peak-to-trough* decline of an investment portfolio.

The peak is achieved when the portfolio reaches a new high value, and drawdown is the period in which the portfolio value is less than the peak. The drawdown is measured from the time a retrenchment begins to the time a new high is reached.

Unlike the traditional standard deviation measure of risk, a drawdown quantifies two equally important factors for investors:

- the size of the loss

- the length of time required to recover the loss

Drawdown calculations allow individual investors to view losses in a more tangible format.

For example, if an individual investor placed their entire portfolio into the S&P 500 Index they could review the historical drawdowns to gain a better understanding of not only the size of previous declines, but also how much *patience* they would require to wait for a full recovery of their account value

This drawdown table shows that patience for a recovery is often measured in years, not months. The amount of time required to produce a loss is rarely proportional to the time required for recovery. For example, you may have to endure an unusually large loss and then have to wait an even longer period of time to recover from it. Alternatively, a loss may be small but the length of time required to recover is long.

Always remember that the amount of time required to recover a loss can be just as significant to your financial success as the size of the loss.

Ten Largest S&P 500 Drawdowns Jan 1970 - Feb 2009

Drawdown	Start	Low	Recovery
-60.66%	Mar 27/00	Feb 24/09	Ongoing
-49.63%	Jan 12/73	Oct 04/74	Oct 07/80
-36.83%	Aug 26/87	Dec 07/87	Jun 05/90
-28.31%	Dec 01/80	Aug 13/82	Jan 07/83
-26.20%	Jan 06/70	May 27/70	Jan 25/71
-20.35%	Jul 17/90	Oct 12/90	Mar 06/91
-20.09%	Jul 20/98	Oct 09/98	Dec 24/98
-19.94%	Sep 22/76	Mar 07/78	Sep 21/79
-17.29%	Feb 14/80	Mar 28/80	Jul 15/80
-14.83%	Oct 11/83	Jul 25/84	Jan 22/85

Source: Bloomberg

The Twisting Road of Recovery and Growth

Financial markets spend long periods of time behaving in a predictable manner, lulling individual investors into a false sense of security only to then randomly and severely deliver punishing negative returns (think: Mandelbrot Rule #1 & 2). The key to investment success is positive long-term compounding (think: I want to go faster). Therefore, the likelihood of experiencing a financial loss should always be of greater concern to you than focusing on a financial advisor's projection of potential future returns.

However, the sales presentations that are used in the financial advice industry will rarely provide information on the historical drawdown of recommended investments, despite this information being easy to obtain for any mutual fund. Why? Because the financial advisor knows that to make you act on a recommendation they need to appeal to your automatic brain and your heuristic biases (think: representativeness, availability and overconfidence biases). Investment presentations are framed around positive projected future rates of return, not historical loses and recovery times.

Your investment decisions need to be evaluated by both considering the potential return and a realistic assessment of the risk of a negative outcome. If a financial advisor does not present all this information to you, then he is not serving your interests.

What Are You Looking At?

Ken had requested a meeting with his financial advisor Larry. Ken had become Larry's client at a large bank-owned brokerage firm after his previous advisor left the industry.

Ken wanted Larry to update him on the progress of the retirement plan that Larry had prepared two years ago. The retirement plan assumed that Ken would always make his maximum allowable RRSP contributions and his investments would produce annual compound 9% returns over the next 10 years.

Ken always had difficulty reading the monthly statements that Larry's firm sent to him. The statements showed the changes in market value of the investments in his account, but they did not include any type of calculation of the investment performance of his portfolio. He was making new contributions to his accounts each month that were being invested together with any cash flow that the existing investments produced. Ken knew that achieving the 9% projected annual return was very important to his portfolio reaching the target value that could support his retirement lifestyle, but he was confused about the actual return that his investments and contributions were achieving.

At the meeting, Larry presented charts of the price histories for each of the eleven mutual funds that Ken held in his account. They all looked very similar, with periods of price increases, price decreases and periods where the prices moved sideways in very narrow ranges. Larry stressed to Ken that, although the prices seemed volatile, most eventually moved higher over longer periods of time.

Ken could see that this was true for some of the chart patterns, but not all of them. He also was unsure about the timeframes of the charts. Some were for one year, some were for five years and some were for ten years. None of these time frames were similar to when Ken initially purchased most of the mutual funds that were held in his account. He also noticed that some of the footnotes that accompanied the charts contained different information. Some were *annualized returns*; others were *total return*, while some were *price only returns*.

He asked Larry to explain what the information in the footnotes meant. Larry acknowledged that the different information used to create the charts did make it difficult to compare them on an "apples to apples" basis, but these were the only charts that the manufacturers of the mutual funds would provide to him. He told Ken not to worry, he reiterated once again that the 9% annual return projection used in his retirement plan was achievable; he just needed to be patient.

Arithmetic or Geometric?

An arithmetic average is the type of average with which most individual investors are familiar.

To calculate the arithmetic average of series, the numbers are added together and that total is then divided by the count of the series.

For example, if you have the numbers 10, 20, 30 and -40, the arithmetic average is 5:

$$[10 + 20 + 30 + (40)] / 4 = 5$$

The arithmetic average should be used when each number in a series is independent of the other numbers. Therefore, using the arithmetic average to calculate the rate of return in your investment portfolio will not be accurate, since the return you received in one period will affect the return you receive in following periods (think: the mathematics of losses). Imagine that the previous number sequence (10, 20, 30 and -40) is the annual rates of return for your investment portfolio over the past four years.

Is your average return the arithmetic average of 5%? It would be nice if that number was correct, but it is not.

These annual investment return numbers are not independent of each other, since the 10% return in first year will affect the amount of capital that you have in your account as you begin the second year.

Therefore, you need to calculate the geometric average of your investment returns to get an accurate understanding of what your average annual return has been over the past four years.

Using annual returns of 10%, 20%, 30% and -40% over the past four years, the geometric average is calculated as:

$[(1 + R_1) \times (1 + R_2) \times (1 + R_3) \times (1 + R_4)]$ - 1

$[(1 + 10\%) \times (1 + 20\%) \times (1 + 30\%) \times (1 + -40\%)]$ - 1

$(1.1 \times 1.2 \times 1.3 \times 0.6) - 1$

$=$ a return of 2.96%

To convert the return over the entire 4-year period into an annualized rate of return, you cannot simply divide by the number of years. Instead, the effective annualized return is:

1 + return for the period to the power of the reciprocal number of years:

$(1 + 2.96\%) \wedge (1 / 4) - 1$

$=$ the annualized rate of return for the period of 0.73%

The arithmetic and geometric average will only be the same when the investment returns that are being averaged are the same for each period. The greater the volatility of the returns, the larger the difference will be between the two alternative ways to calculate the averages.

The arithmetic average is always higher than the geometric average. Therefore the arithmetic average return is usually what is used in advertisements for mutual funds and for charts that show short timeframes. You should always read the fine print so you understand which method was used to calculate the return.

Linear or Log?

Charts are frequently used as a way to represent numerical financial market data. The visual display is intended to ease your understanding of large quantities of data and assist in identifying any relationships that may be present.

Financial charts will generally use two different forms of price scales:

A logarithmic scale is a measurement that uses the logarithm of a quantity, rather than the quantity itself. The result is that the plots on the charts are not equally spaced by distance; instead they are equally spaced as percentages. Therefore, the distance between five and ten is the same as the distance between ten and twenty. Therefore, on a chart a price bar representing a 50% gain will be the same size no matter where it appears. Below is a chart of the monthly total returns of the S&P/TSX Composite Index produced on a logarithmic scale.

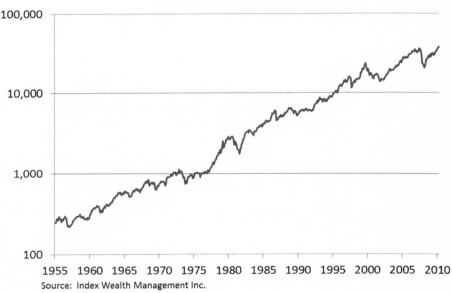

S&P/TSX Monthly Total Return

Source: Index Wealth Management Inc.

A linear scale uses plots that are spaced so that the distance between the plots is equal. Therefore, each value is represented by the same vertical distance on the chart, regardless of the price level when the change occurs. A linear price scale will disregard the fact that a $5 move is more substantial when the price of an asset is $10 than when the price of the asset is $50. The price change will be plotted on the chart as being the same distance, even though the earlier $5 increase is equal to a 50% increase, while the latter is only a 10% increase. Below is a chart of the monthly total returns of the S&P/TSX Composite Index produced on a linear scale.

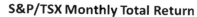

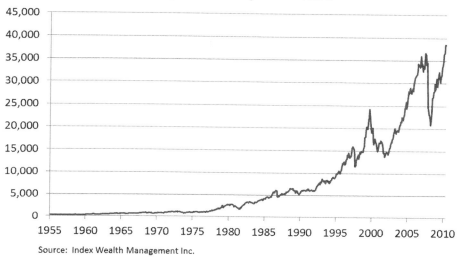

Source: Index Wealth Management Inc.

When comparing these two chart types, a logarithmic scale puts an equal weight on each price movement, which makes large price changes appear much more dramatic. For this reason, a logarithmic scale is used most often by the financial advice industry to display compound growth.

You need to be aware that the use of a linear scale can sometimes be used to change the frame perception you receive from a chart. As a result, compound growth rates may not be discernable when placed on a linear scale.

Mountain Climbing

Below is a common form of chart that illustrates the long-term return performance for the S&P/TSX Composite Index. This is the most frequently used form of chart, which plots price movements against time. They are sometimes referred to as *mountain charts*, because of the visual shape the data creates.

The chart below is based on the monthly compounded total return of the index and is shown in a log scale.

S&P/TSX Monthly Total Return

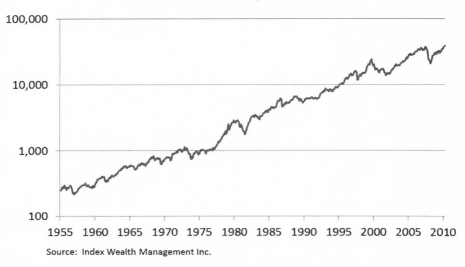

Source: Index Wealth Management Inc.

These charts are also often used by financial advisors to illustrate price move-ments, in an attempt to illustrate past investment returns. They are also ripe with misinformation:

- The charts show nominal rather than real rates of return (think: money illusion).

Nominal returns only use current market value, without taking into account the effects that inflation has on the purchasing power of an investment. You should focus on inflation adjusted, or *real* returns, since this is what you need to maintain the purchasing power of your investments.

The chart below shows a comparison of real vs. nominal total monthly com-pounded total returns for the S&P/TSX Composite Index. Inflation data is based on the monthly changes in the Consumer Price Index (CPI).

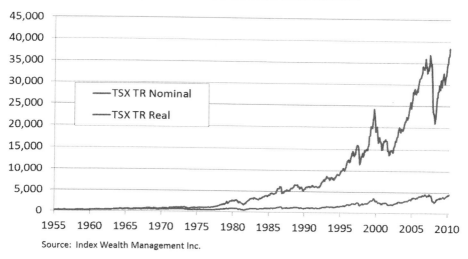

S&P/TSX Nominal vs. Real Total Returns

Source: Index Wealth Management Inc.

Financial advisors will often encourage you to purchase stocks as a hedge against inflation (which is not always the relationship over short time horizons). However, they will likely show you only nominal return charts. Charts that use nominal returns are designed to appeal to your money illusion bias, since the nominal returns appear greater than real returns.

- The charts show annualized returns.

An annual rate of return is a single-period return, such as the return on an investment over one year, say, January 1st through December 31st.

An annualized rate of return is the return on an investment over a period other than one year (think: one month or three years) that is then adjusted to give a comparable one-year return. For instance, a one-month return of 2% could be expressed as an annualized rate of return of 24%.

Annualized returns provide the mistaken impression that *risk* is reduced over longer time horizons, since variations in annualized returns over long periods seem to disappear.

The chart below shows the monthly compounded annualized total return of the S&P/TSX Composite Index in a log scale.

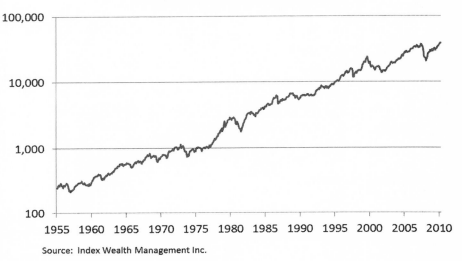

S&P/TSX Annualized Total Return

Source: Index Wealth Management Inc.

The historic October 19th, 1987 decline is something that you need to search for because it doesn't appear significant by viewing the chart.

The total return of an investment is what matters for individual investors, not the annualized return. The chart below shows the one year rolling returns, rather than the annualized returns, and should provide you with a much different impression about the volatility of returns that have been produced by the S&P/TSX Composite Index. The variation in the returns for each one-year period is enormous when the smoothing effect of annualizing the return is removed.

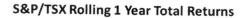

S&P/TSX Rolling 1 Year Total Returns

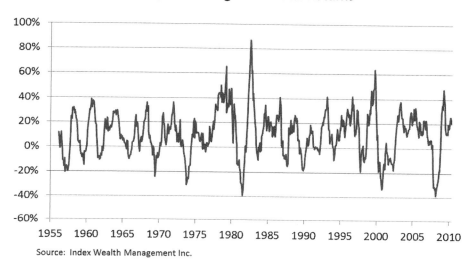

Source: Index Wealth Management Inc.

- The chart only provides an accurate impression of the investment return if it is held for the entire time horizon.

Other than for the sake of simplicity, there is no theoretical reason why investment returns should be shown as one-year time horizons that end with the calendar year. In order for you to have received the rate of return that a chart is illustrating, you must invest at the start of the timeframe and stay invested until the end of the period. No additional selling is allowed over this period, or the return you receive will be different. This is a very unrealistic assumption for most individual investors, especially when viewing charts that frequently have timeframes greater than ten years.

- If a chart shows a total rate of return, then it assumes the reinvestment of all dividend and capital gain distributions.

The chart below shows the cumulative return of a $1 investment in the S&P/TSX Composite Index from January 1, 1956 to March 31, 2010 on a price-only basis and on a total return basis. The total return includes the reinvestment of *all* dividends since the start of the period. Total return charts are usually used to illustrate long-term investment returns because they are much more visually appealing than price only charts.

S&P/TSX Price vs. Total Return

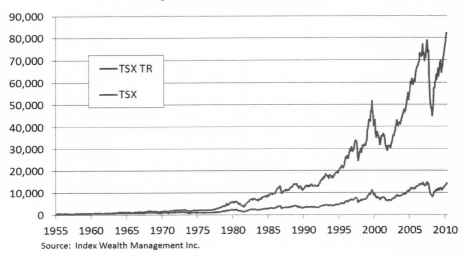

Source: Index Wealth Management Inc.

If the dividends that were paid were spent rather than reinvested, then the rate of return will be substantially lower than what is usually shown in a chart as being representative of a historical investment return.

• Charts do not account for taxes.

Charts that show total returns require the reinvestment of the entire amounts that are distributed, even if you are required to pay tax on the distributions.

Dividends, interest and capital gains are taxable in the year in which they are received unless the investment is held in a tax sheltered account, such as a RRSP or TFSA. Therefore, for this reinvestment to occur, it means that the tax payable on the distributed income has to be paid from another source of funds. Even if you faithfully reinvested every distribution you received, your total rate of return would be lower than what the chart indicates. Why? Since the amount you pay in tax on the distributions must come from withdrawing funds from another source, an accurate return calculation requires that you must account for this additional capital used to pay tax.

Charts also do not make any allowance for the capital gains taxes that would be payable on the growth of an investment.

A $1 investment that grew to $ 82,055 would require the payment of capital gain taxes if you sold some or all of the investment at the end of the time horizon.

Dollar Cost Averaging

Mary had just inherited $100,000, so she called John for an appointment. John is a financial planner and had been advising Mary regarding her RRSP investments over the last decade. Once each year, John would call Mary during the last week of the RRSP contribution season and urge her to meet with him. During the meetings, John would present Mary with a list of mutual funds that had performed well over the past year and help her select one that he believed would be a suitable investment for this year's contribution. Mary now had a dozen different funds in her account and none of the funds ever seemed to live up to their track record after she made the investments.

At the meeting, John provided Mary with a list of five new mutual funds that he believed would be excellent additions to her portfolio. Mary told John that she was apprehensive about investing the entire amount of the inheritance all at one time. She thought that the market had been very strong lately, so she would prefer to wait for the market to correct (think: representativeness) so that she could invest at lower prices.

John believed that she should begin investing immediately, so he recommended a strategy called *dollar cost averaging*. He said it would remove the guessing of when to buy low and sell high, since mutual fund prices will always fluctuate. Mary would buy more units when prices are low and she would also buy fewer units when prices are high. Therefore, the strategy would lower the average cost of her investments.

Mary thought the idea made sense, since she always felt bad (think: regret) after the mutual funds she purchased in her RRSP seemed to decline after she purchased them.

Mary did wonder why John never recommended this strategy for her RRSP contributions, rather than waiting until the deadline to make a lump sum investment. She never asked the question, because John was busy preparing the paperwork for monthly investments of $5,000 that would be divided equally between five new mutual funds. Mary felt better knowing that she could use the volatility of the market to her advantage.

Dollar cost averaging is an investment strategy that promotes gradually investing proportional dollar amounts into a mutual fund over a specific timeframe, rather than investing in one lump sum purchase. The strategy is typically recommended for individual investors when purchasing units of a mutual fund and is frequently touted by the financial advice industry as a way of enhancing investment performance.

The rationale for using this strategy is that, by investing only a fixed amount (i.e. $500) each month, fewer units of a mutual fund are purchased when prices are high, and more units are purchased when prices are low. The result is that the average cost per unit is lowered and the risk of making a single large purchase at a high price which is then followed by a decline is reduced.

This strategy is an attempt to overcome your loss aversion heuristic bias. It frames the investment decision in such a way that you will act today, rather than wait and see what will happen with future prices.

As the dollar cost averaging strategy begins and unit prices fluctuate, any regret you feel from your investment declining below the initial purchase price is now framed as an *opportunity* to buy more units at a lower cost.

Any mutual funds that are recommended by your financial advisor are projected to increase in value over time. Have you ever been told by an advisor that a recommended investment will decline over the long term?

You will usually be shown a chart of a fund with an enviable performance track record that illustrates a history of positive returns. However, you will also be cautioned that the investment can experience short-term price fluctuations. Therefore, the risk associated with making a lump sum purchase is that poor timing might result in a large purchase during a short- term price increase, resulting in the number of units purchased being less than if you bought at lower prices.

The concept of dollar cost averaging seems logical, but what really is the *risk* associated with a single lump-sum purchase?

Example 1: Increasing Fund Prices

Over the course of a year, you make monthly $500 purchases of mutual fund units. The units are initially purchased at $10 per share and then increase in price by 1% per month:

	Investment	Price / Share	Shares Purchased
January	$ 500.00	$10.00	50.00
February	$ 500.00	$10.10	49.51
March	$ 500.00	$10.20	49.02
April	$ 500.00	$10.30	48.54
May	$ 500.00	$10.41	48.03
June	$ 500.00	$10.51	47.57
July	$ 500.00	$10.62	47.08
August	$ 500.00	$10.72	46.64
September	$ 500.00	$10.83	46.17
October	$ 500.00	$10.94	45.70
November	$ 500.00	$11.05	45.25
December	$ 500.00	$11.16	44.80
Total	$6,000.00		568.31

In this example, you purchased 568.31 units for $6,000, or an average cost of $10.56 per unit. Alternatively, you could have purchased 600 units of the mutual fund in January at $10 per unit and been better off.

Example 2: Decreasing Fund Prices

Over the course of the next year, you make monthly $500 purchases of a different mutual fund. The units are initially purchased at $10 per share and then decrease in price by 1% per month:

	Investment	Price / Share	Shares Purchased
January	$ 500.00	$10.00	50.00
February	$ 500.00	$9.90	50.51
March	$ 500.00	$9.80	51.02
April	$ 500.00	$9.70	51.55
May	$ 500.00	$9.61	52.03
June	$ 500.00	$9.51	52.58
July	$ 500.00	$9.41	53.14
August	$ 500.00	$9.32	53.65
September	$ 500.00	$9.23	54.17
October	$ 500.00	$9.14	54.71
November	$ 500.00	$9.04	55.31
December	$ 500.00	$8.95	55.87
Total	$6,000.00		634.48

In this second example, you purchased 634.48 units for $6,000, or an average cost of $9.46 per unit. Here, dollar cost averaging seems to work, since you would hold only 600 units if you made a lump-sum purchase in January.

The first example shows that when prices are increasing over time, dollar cost averaging results in higher average prices compared to an initial lump sum purchase. Since financial market prices tend to trend upwards over long time horizons, investing in the market today tends to be better than waiting until tomorrow. Therefore, dollar cost averaging will always face a statistical headwind, because it is likely that the average price tomorrow will be higher than it is today.

If this is true, then why do financial advisors still advocate the approach?

The main argument used (think: misinformation) in the sale of mutual funds that advocate this strategy, is that gradual investing implicitly reduces volatility at a minimal expense to long term returns. In other words, dollar cost averaging acts to reduce the volatility of returns as prices fluctuate between advances and declines. Therefore, using this approach should result in you purchasing units of a mutual fund at a better than average historical price. This was the outcome that was shown in the second example.

However, this outcome is meaningless since it is the future price of the fund, not the past prices that will determine your profit or loss. What matters is the future price at which you sell your mutual fund investment, since the value of the fund will either be above or below your historical average purchase price. This is true whether your average cost is the result of dollar cost averaging or a lump sum purchase. Even with financial market prices generally trending higher over time, there is no guarantee that on the day you need to sell some or all of your investment, the market price won't be lower than your historical average cost.

A research study (Constantinides 1979) denounced the dollar cost averaging investment strategy as pure myth as long as 30 years ago by highlighting the inefficiencies of the strategy.[93]

Additional studies (Bacon and Ainina 1997) using historical returns from 1926 to 1993 for U.S. bonds concluded that an individual investor would have received higher returns with a simple buy-and-hold or lump sum investment strategy, as opposed to dollar cost averaging. In addition, it did not meaningfully reduce risk when compared to other strategies, including a completely random investment strategy.[94]

Dollar cost averaging also fails when it is compared to both a buy- and- hold and a constant rebalancing approach. Constant rebalancing requires buying more of the risky asset when prices have fallen, and selling when prices have risen at the end of pre-established periods. Mandel and Knight (1993) conducted a study using three sample investor types for analysis, and monthly returns from 1962 to 1992 for U.S. financial markets:

- A very risk averse investor (10% in stocks)

- A average risk investor (50% in stocks, 50% in bonds)

- A above average risk investor (90% stocks)

The study showed that the dollar cost averaging approach produced the poorest results of the three approaches that were evaluated. The authors concluded:

"Our results strongly imply that the additional cost and effort associated with dollar cost averaging cannot be justified for any investor, regardless of degree of risk aversion. With the possible exception of its promoters, nobody gains from dollar cost averaging."[95]

I believe the conclusion by the researchers is especially relevant because it clearly states that the financial advice industry is promoting an investment strategy that only benefits itself.

Dollar cost averaging allows the financial advice industry to frame future invest-ment price declines as *buying opportunities* rather than losses. Therefore, you are more likely to be convinced to buy today and to keep buying, even as prices decline in the future.

Other People's Money

Darlene and Darryl are having their annual investment meeting with their financial advisor. They met Doug five years ago when he first began working in the life insur-ance industry and they needed to purchase some term insurance. When he received his mutual fund sales licence, he advised them to set up a monthly investment program with the goal of saving enough capital to provide savings for their retirement. The strategy was designed to take advantage of dollar cost averaging by investing in several of the mutual funds that were managed by his insurance company employer. Doug had recommended investing in the funds based on their excellent track records.

In the meeting, Darlene and Darryl told Doug that they were concerned about the performance of their investments. Every month they were saving some of their income to build a nest egg for retirement, but they hadn't seen any growth in the value of their account. Doug confirmed that the market value of their account was substan-tially below what he projected it would be when they began their investment program five years ago. The prices of the mutual funds he recommended initially rose when they began to invest, only to decline for the past several years as financial markets performed poorly. The prices were now almost exactly the same as they were five years ago and they only had ten years left until retirement. Did this not mean that they would require a higher return from their investments to make up for the last five years that have been lost, so that they could still meet their retirement goal (think: the mathematics of losses)?

Doug seemed to understand their concerns. They were very similar to what he was hearing from many of his clients. He was surprised that the track records of the funds he recommended did not live up to the 9% annual return projection that he believed was reasonable for the next fifteen years. After all, that was the track record that the funds produced for the previous two years before he made the recommendation.

Doug told the couple that the timing of their meeting was very good, since his firm had just begun to encourage him to tell his clients about a new investment strategy that they were now offering. The program is based on the concept of using other people's money to achieve their retirement goals.

How would this strategy work?

Doug explained that, to achieve their investment goals sooner, Darlene and Darryl didn't need to increase the rate of return of their investments; rather they just needed to increase the capital value of their account today to rely on the effects of compounding. They could do this by borrowing money that could then be used to buy more mutual funds. Doug's employer offered a leveraged investment program that would allow clients to make new mutual fund purchases that were two, three or even four times the amount of capital that they currently had in their account. This meant that they could increase the amount of their $50,000 investment by an additional $150,000 to $200,000. Doug's firm would lend them the money for the new purchases and then use the mutual funds as collateral for the loan. The loan payments could be made equal to what they were currently contributing to their investment account, so that their out of pocket expenses would be the same. As an added benefit, the interest they would pay on the loan would be tax deductible.

Darlene and Darryl thought the concept sounded very appealing, but they had heard about this type of strategy before and were sure that borrowing to invest can increase the *risk* they were taking. They had seen the prices of their mutual funds swing by large amounts each year and this volatility made them feel uncomfortable.

Doug reminded them that they had borrowed in the past to invest, when they bought their house, and that was a much larger dollar amount. Also, the interest they paid on their mortgage was not tax deductible.

Doug did acknowledge that borrowing to invest in mutual funds involved a greater degree of risk than their current dollar cost averaging saving program, but they needed to understand that *risk in financial markets decreases the longer the time frame they have to hold their investments.*

In their current strategy of using their monthly savings to purchase mutual funds, their gain or loss would be equal to the gain or loss that was produced by these investments. However, if they borrowed money to invest, the gain or loss they would experience would be greater relative to the performance of the funds.

For example, if at the end of ten years the $50,000 current market value of their account declined in value to $40,000, they would lose $10,000. However, if they borrowed $50,000 at a rate of 6.0% and the account declines by the same $10,000 at the end of ten years, they would be in a worse financial position. They would have lost $10,000 of their original capital, they would still have to repay the $50,000 loan and they would have also paid $30,000 in loan interest over the ten years. In other words, they would have lost $40,000 with the leveraged strategy, rather than $10,000 with their existing dollar cost averaging strategy.

Doug told Darlene and Darryl that although there is the potential for increased losses, he believed that to help understand how this strategy might perform in the future, it can be useful to look at how this strategy would have performed in the past.

Doug produced a table of returns for the S&P/TSX Total Return Index from 1956 to 2004. The table compared a leverage strategy for an investor with a 35% marginal tax rate who borrowed and invested $50,000 for ten years and paid interest at the prevailing prime lending rate plus 1.25%.

The table showed the maximum, medium and minimum amounts that an investor would have received by using each strategy. The minimum represented the amount earned after taxes and the loan repayment if they had invested during the worst 10-year period. While the maximum represented the amount earned after taxes and loan repayment if they had invested during the best 10-year period.

Leverage Strategy:
Maximum: $154,500
Median: $30,190
Minimum ($11,231)

Non Leverage Strategy
Maximum: $65,008
Median: $15,063
Minimum: $3,699

Doug used the information in the table to illustrate (think: framing) that, although the highs are higher and the lows are lower with the leverage strategy, the median and maximum returns would have been significantly higher with a leverage strategy than with a non-leverage strategy.

Darlene and Darryl looked at the numbers and they confirmed what Doug had said. Not only were the median and maximum returns higher; the minimum leveraged return loss of $11,231 did not appear to be that much more than the paltry $3,699 return of the non-leverage strategy.

These historical 10-year rolling average rates of return confirmed what Doug had said: *risk in financial markets decreases the longer the time frame they have to hold their investments*. In fact, Darryl and Darlene now believed that they could tolerate more *risk* in their investments, so they agreed to participate in the leveraged program by borrowing $150,000 to leverage 3:1 to maximize the amount of capital that their account could grow to when they needed to retire. They passed on the offer of 4:1 leverage, because they didn't want to be too aggressive, but they felt comfortable knowing that the leverage they used to buy their first home was close to 10:1 and that turned out well!

Doug began to complete the loan application form and the risk disclosure form that is required by securities regulations to prove that Darlene and Darryl understood the *risk* of entering into the leveraged investment strategy.

Having Your Cake and Eating It Too!

Leveraging is borrowing money to invest. It is often framed by the financial industry as using other people's money to help you achieve your financial goals sooner.

In a traditional investing program you contribute savings (usually monthly or annually) to an account. These funds are then used to purchase investments in the same frequency as when new capital is added. The objective is that your selected investments will then compound over time to allow you to achieve your goal, such as providing an income when you reach retirement.

In a leveraged investing program, you make a single large investment when you begin the strategy, by borrowing money. Rather than contributing savings to the account, you instead use these funds to make monthly or annual payments to service the loan. The payments can service either the interest or the interest and principal of the loan, but it is frequently recommended that interest-only payments be made to maximize the amount that can be borrowed to make the initial investment.

Making the loan servicing payments equivalent to what you would have contributed by way of savings frames a savings program and a leveraged strategy as having the same out of pocket costs, but the leveraged strategy has the potential to generate larger returns.

Collateral for the loan can be either the investments that are purchased or another asset, such as your home. Some financial institutions market loan programs that allow for leverage up to 4:1.

The financial industry promotes two main advantages of a leveraged investment strategy:

- Increased compound returns from having the largest possible amount of capital growing for the longest possible time. If Darlene and Darryl have a 10-year investment horizon and plan to make regular contributions each year then, by using a traditional saving strategy, only the contribution they make in the first year will compound for the entire 10 years. The contributions they make in year two will only have nine years to grow, etc. Therefore, with a leveraged strategy a large amount of capital is invested initially so that they receive the benefit of compounding for the entire ten years, which can result in better investment results over the long term.

- The amount of *risk* involved in a leveraged strategy decreases as the investment horizon increases. This is because the return of stocks varies widely from year to year, but these fluctuations tend to even out over the longer term.[96]

Misinformation, Misunderstanding and Overconfidence

It is generally understood by most financial advisors and many individual investors that borrowing money to invest does involve a larger degree of risk than an investment strategy that is based on investing only saved capital. Securities regulations require that investors receive and acknowledge a risk disclosure that states:

"Using borrowed money to finance the purchase of securities involves greater risk than a purchase using cash resources only. If you borrow money to purchase securities, your responsibility to repay the loan and pay interest as required by its terms remains the same even if the value of the securities purchased declines".[97]

At the same time this risk is disclosed, it is also downplayed by the often repeated financial industry mantra: *investing for the long term reduces risk.*

It is common sense that if a financial advisor actually thought the risk was greater than the potential returns of the strategy they would not recommended it to clients.

But does investing for the long term actually reduce the risk of a leveraged investment strategy?

Is the Past Relevant?

As part of the leveraged investment strategy sales presentation a potential investor is frequently shown historical investment performance returns that are used to support the rationale of the strategy. However, more often than not, they do not show the actual performance history of the security(s) that the financial advisor will ultimately be recommending as the investment for the leveraged strategy. Reviewing the historical returns of the S&P/TSX Composite Index has no relevance if you are not making an investment in a security that is designed to replicate the performance of this Index (think: misinformation). A financial advisor will likely be recommending that you invest in actively managed mutual funds so that they can be compensated (think: MER). Therefore, it is also very likely that the investment return you receive from the mutual funds will be different than the return of the financial index past performance histories (think: the myth of active management).

The Path You Take Will Determine if You Actually Arrive

The concept of *time diversification* is rooted in the belief that financial market risk can be reduced by investing for a long time horizon. Therefore, if you have enough patience, you can always wait for prices to recover from losses.

Therefore, a leveraged investment strategy relies on a definition of risk that is based solely on the likelihood of a loss being present only at the very end of the investment horizon. This definition of risk ignores the sequence of returns (positive and negative) that can occur at any time between the time you make the initial investment and just prior to when your planned investment horizon ends.

Does this sequence of returns really matter, even for a long-term investor who is prepared to ride out the highs and lows?

A leveraged investment program will always have a maximum loss threshold that is determined by the size of the loan compared to the size of the underlying investment collateral that is securing the loan (think: loan to equity ratio). There are limits imposed under the loan agreement regarding the value of collateral that must always be in place to allow the loan agreement to continue. If the collateral declines below a specified ratio, then you are required to restore that ratio by either adding more collateral or reducing the amount of the loan balance. The requirement to add more collateral is commonly referred to as a *margin call*.

For example, if Darlene and Darryl have $50,000 of saved capital and want to enter a 3:1 leveraged investment program, then they will borrow another $150,000 for a total investment of $200,000.

The maximum loan value is $150,000 based on equity of $50,000. Therefore to maintain the $150,000 loan, they must always have $50,000 of their own equity as collateral.

What happens when the value of their investment fluctuates?

Scenario one

The total market value of their investments increases by 10% to $220,000

Original Equity:	$ 50,000
Original Market Value	$200,000
Current Market Value	$220,000
Less: Loan Value	$150,000
Margin Excess	$ 70,000

Scenario two

The total market value of the investment decreases by 10% to $180,000

Original Equity:	$ 50,000
Original Market Value	$200,000
Current Market Value	$180,000
Less: Loan Value	$150,000
Margin Excess	$ 30,000

A 3:1 leveraged strategy (75% loan: equity) typically has a margin call when the loan: equity increase to 95%.[98]

The loan to equity ratio determines when the margin call will occur and acts as a maximum loss threshold for the leverage program to continue.

The sequence of returns Darlene and Darryl experience over their investment time horizon are very important, since the probability of receiving a margin call depends on this sequence. This *within-horizon risk* is actually a larger risk than the *end-of-horizon risk*, which is the only focus of a leveraged investment strategy presentation.[99]

The diagram below illustrates the difference between risk based on ending outcomes and risk based on outcomes that occur from a sequence of return paths.

Each line represents four possible return sequences for a $100 investment. The horizontal line at 90% represents a loss threshold of 10%. Only one of the five paths breaches this threshold *at the end* of the horizon. Therefore, using only the end of horizon risk assumes that the likelihood of a 10% loss is 1 in 5, or 20%.

However, four of the five paths breach the loss threshold at some point during the investment horizon and only three of the four paths subsequently recover. Therefore, since the sequence of the returns that occur along the way to the end of the horizon does matter, the likelihood of a 10% loss is actually four in five, or 80%.

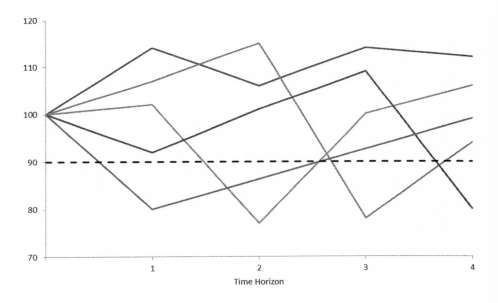

The estimate of the probability of loss from the start of the strategy to any point in time throughout the investment horizon is path dependent. You cannot ignore the specific sequence of returns that lead to the final result, since some sequences that eventually finish above the threshold will have, at some point along the way, also breached the loss threshold. While the likelihood of an end-of-horizon loss diminishes with time, the likelihood of a within-horizon loss never diminishes as a function of the length of the horizon. Therefore, the likelihood of a *fat tail* occurring that breaches the maximum loss threshold is just as likely to occur in the first month of a 10-year investment horizon as it is to occur in the last month.

The occurrence of the first breach in the loss threshold is really all that matters, because this causes the investment strategy to stop unless more capital is added. If the strategy is forced to close, then the end-of-horizon loss probabilities do not have any relevance. Knowing the frequency, magnitude and duration of losses (think: drawdowns) that have previously occurred are very useful to Darlene and Darryl when they are evaluating the risk and reward trade-off of a leveraged investment strategy.

The strategy is sold to individual investors by framing the outcomes of future investment prices as being similar to that of tossing a coin. The assumption is that the probability of a future upward movement in price is equal to the probability of a future downward movement, so that future gains and futures losses in prices will tend to offset each other in the long run. This reasoning assumes that a -5% return is certain to be followed by a +5% return and a 5% return is certain to be followed by a -5% return. This type of serial correlation would eliminate all uncertainty, but it has no resemblance to the random sequence of returns that are produced by financial markets. The *law of averages* does not ensure a concept of fairness in financial markets so that investment returns will always even out (think: gambler's fallacy).

Leveraged investing is more akin to a coin tossing game that continues for an unknown time frame and then stops randomly. If you begin playing this game and win $1 for each head and lose $1 for each tail, at some point in the game you may have a run of bad luck and will lose several dollars in succession. If these losses cause you to run out of money, the game will end. If you have a series of losses (think: volatility tends to cluster) on a leveraged investment, you are required to add more capital to meet the margin requirement or your investment position will be sold. If at some point you do not have the capital to meet a margin call, you are forced out of the game and cannot recoup your loss.

The probabilities of success with a leveraged investment strategy depend on the sequence of your investment returns and the amount of capital you have available to allow you to continue throughout your entire investment horizon.

Russian Irony

Let's play another coin tossing game. In this game, the rules are very simple:

- You pay a fixed fee to enter the game.

- Each time a toss is heads you win the amount of the jackpot.

- The game will continue until a tail appears and then it ends.

The jackpot starts at $1 and will double every time a head appears. When the game ends with the toss of a tail, you claim whatever amount is in the jackpot.

Therefore, you would win:

- One dollar if a tail appears on the first toss.

- Two dollars if a head appears on the first toss and then a tail on the second.

- Four dollars if a head appears on the first two tosses and a tail on the third.

- Eight dollars if a head appears on the first three tosses and a tail on the fourth, etc.

Given that the worst possible outcome for you is $1, what would be the maximum amount you would be willing to pay as an entry fee to play this game?

To answer this question, you need to calculate the *expected value* that you would receive by playing the game. The expected value of the game is the sum of the expected payoffs of all the sequences. Since the expected payoff of each possible sequence cannot be less than $1 and there are an infinite number of possible sequences, then this makes the expected value an infinite number of dollars.

By playing this game you should always come out ahead in the long run, no matter how much you pay as a fixed fee to enter the game. There is no possibility of a margin call. Although a large jackpot will be paid only on rare occasions, it will be much larger than the amount of money that you paid to have the opportunity to play the game. Therefore, if you are a rational individual you would play the game at any price. This game is commonly referred to as the St. Petersburg Paradox.

The typical *heads you win, tails I lose* game that we have all played allows for the calculation of an expected value that is based on the 50/50 chance of either a head or tail appearing on each toss. Therefore, the optimal fixed entry fee to pay to enter this game is 50 cents for a minimum jackpot of $1.

The coin toss game that underlies the St. Petersburg paradox is a fractal game that follows a power law distribution. The game offers the possibility of huge jackpots, with 40 heads in a row paying $1.1 trillion. However, 50% of the time the game pays only $2, and 75% of the time the jackpot is $4 or less. Your chances of winning a jackpot larger than $25 are less than 1 in 25.

There is a high probability of receiving a small jackpot, a medium probability of receiving a larger jackpot, but on an extremely rare occasion, you could win a jackpot of more money than you could imagine. These frequent small amounts, somewhat less frequent medium amounts and very infrequent large amounts are similar to the small, medium and large pieces in a fractal object. There is no single average value that can be considered to be the usual value of the winnings from each game.

Instead, when you play this fractal coin toss game your winnings per game will keep increasing. The more you play, the more you will win. A string of heads will produce a large jackpot, which will continue to increase the average winnings per game. Therefore, the average expected value of the game will always increase.

The St. Petersburg Paradox presents a situation that requires decision making based on naïve rules that do not consider the expected value of the outcome. This results in a recommended strategy that very few individuals would accept.

A study (Hacking 1980) of this fractal coin tossing game, asked participants how much of a fixed entry fee they would be willing to pay to play the game. The answer was that very few would be willing to pay even $25.[100]

Why would this be?

The answer to the question lies in the *theory of diminishing marginal utility*.

The theory states that the extra utility obtained from consuming a good decreases as the quantity consumed increases. The result is that each additional good consumed is less satisfying than the previous one. Therefore, the determination of the value of an item is not based solely on the price, but rather on the utility it yields.

Think about two individuals:

✓ One has $1,000 in savings

✓ The other has $1,000,000 in savings

They each win a lottery with a prize of $1,000. The dollar amount they receive is exactly the same, but will the prize have the same significance to each individual? Probably not, since it will double one individual's savings, while not making much of a difference to the other.

The Paradox of Leveraged Investing

If you believe that investing all your savings in the equity market for a one-year time horizon is an acceptable risk, would you also then choose to make the same investment over a 10-year time horizon? What circumstances would have to change in the future to make you believe that this investment was now unacceptable?

Imagine that you have total current savings of $50,000. Based on your tolerance for risk, the asset allocation you have selected for your investments is 100% equities. Your investments are incredibly successful and over the next five years the market value of your portfolio increases to $1,000,000. Would you now change your portfolio's asset allocation for the next five years to make it a little less volatile, in the hope of preserving some of your gains, or would you leave it unchanged?

Very few individuals have tolerances for risk that are independent of wealth. However, a leveraged investing strategy is based on the false premise that an investor's risk tolerances will always remain constant and will not be influenced by their total wealth.

Therefore, the individual investor who has a $1,000,000 portfolio must view a potential loss of 25% in the last year of his investment time horizon as being equally acceptable to a potential 25% loss on a $50,000 portfolio in the first year of the investment time horizon. My experience working with individual investors has taught me that this is not true.

Individual investors are *not* indifferent between a $250,000 loss in the year they will begin their retirement and a $12,500 loss when they start an investment program with a long time horizon remaining until retirement. You should not accept an investment risk unless that risk is acceptable to you regardless of the time horizon. Therefore, unless you find a potential loss acceptable at any point during the *entire* leveraged investment strategy time horizon, you should not make the investment.

All individual investors are risk adverse. They differ only in their degree of risk aversion and in how their risk tolerance changes as their wealth increases and decreases.

The St. Petersburg paradox demonstrates that if you find the risk of a bet unacceptable, you should also find the risk that is present in a series of the exact same bets unacceptable as well, even if the potential reward of the bet is enormous. The time diversification risk reduction strategy that underlies the premise of why you should increase your risk tolerance by borrowing to invest, requires that an individual with a 10-year time horizon keep the *same* asset allocation for all ten years. Therefore, it is based on the flawed assumption that your risk tolerance never changes and it is completely independent of changes in your total wealth.

A study (Samuelson 1966) demonstrated that the *decrease* in the probability of a loss is exactly offset by the *increase* in the potential magnitude of loss. Therefore, instead of increasing the risk of your portfolio based upon a long-term time horizon, you should select an asset allocation based upon the amount of risk you are willing to take in any one-year time horizon. In most circumstances, the risk profile of your single year time horizon portfolio will be much more conservative than a risk profile you would assume based upon a 10-year time horizon. [101]

The financial advice industry shows individual investors a measure of risk that is expressed in percentage terms, when the focus should be on risk measured in dollar amounts (think: misinformation). The increasing scale of the potential dollar losses is what is important. Focusing only on a reduced probability of end-of-horizon losses ignores the crucial fact that the *probability of loss in any one year is the same in each year of the investment horizon.* If a large loss comes near the end of the investment horizon, the dollar amount of the loss would be severe and most likely would not be recovered (think: the mathematics of losses).

Why Is Leveraged Investing Recommended?

A financial advisor's recommendation to embark on a leveraged investment odyssey contains the following implied assumptions:

- You are not likely to experience a return path that crosses a loss threshold that results in a margin call.

- You will achieve a rate of return that is sufficient to cover the interest you are paying on the loan.

- The mutual fund(s) you are being sold will achieve an additional rate of return that compensates you for the incredible amount of uncertainty (not risk) you are accepting by utilizing the strategy.

- You will not experience a period of severe volatility that tempts you to either reduce the amount of leverage or change the asset allocation of your portfolio.

I would suggest that most individual investors are very unlikely to achieve all of these objectives.

So why then is the strategy promoted by the financial advice industry?

The obvious answer is that advisors who are paid by commission can make double or triple the income today by increasing the amount of capital their clients have available for investment.

Think again about the example of Darlene and Darryl who have $50,000 of existing mutual fund investments and have now decided to borrow another $150,000 to invest in more mutual funds.

Existing Portfolio

$50,000 of existing mutual funds

0.50% trailer fee, or $250, paid annually to the advisor.

New Portfolio

$150,000 of new mutual funds

5% DSC commission is paid to the advisor = $7,000

0.50% trailer fee, or $750, paid annually to the advisor.

The total annual trailer fee from $200,000 of mutual funds is now $1,000

A lender, who may also be an associate company of the advisor's employer, also makes money:

Interest only $150,000 loan at 5% interest = $7,500

Over the 10-year investment horizon that total interest will be $75,000.

CHAPTER 6

YOUR WAY FORWARD: A BETTER APPROACH TO FINANCIAL MARKET UNCERTAINTY

"Even the most brilliant mathematical geniuses will never be able to tell us what the future holds. In the end, what matters is the quality of our decisions in the face of uncertainty."

Peter L. Bernstein, economist and money manager

Route Step March

The Millennium Bridge is a lateral suspension bridge that extends from London's financial district (which is ironic in itself) over the River Thames. Prior to its opening on June 10th, 2000 engineers called it "an absolute statement of our capabilities at the beginning of the 21st century."[102]

The bridge had been designed to surpass all safety standards and was rigorously tested to withstand hazards such as weight and wind. However, on the opening day, as tens of thousands of pedestrians began to cross over it, the bridge began to produce an unexpected sideways sway. As the swaying intensified each person began to adjust their cadence to maintain balance and this resulted in an unintentional synchronization of their footsteps that caused the motion to worsen. The bridge had to be closed until a solution could be found.

It was subsequently discovered that the bridge movement was caused by the sideways force we all produce when we walk. The bridge reopened in 2002 after engineers refitted it with dampers to absorb the motion.

Militaries have understood for over a century that troops marching in step can create a force that affects the stability of some types of bridges. Therefore, it is standard practice for soldiers to break step at bridge crossings under the command "route step march". This allows the soldiers to walk without being in step.[103]

The consequences of synchronized footsteps on a bridge are a risk that is understood by the military. Yet engineers did not account for this occurrence when they were testing the millennium bridge design for what they believed was every known type of uncertainty that may present a danger.

Risk = Uncertainty x Consequence

Modern Portfolio Theory and much of the rhetoric that is produced by the financial advice industry is grounded in the false belief that financial market uncertainty can always be tamed. Better financial models, diversification across asset classes and active portfolio management are trumpeted as effective ways to conquer financial market *risk*. This belief conveniently ignores the continual boom and bust of prices in financial markets and the resulting unpleasant consequences that are experienced by individual investors. The standard advice of *be patient and prices will eventually recover* is cold comfort to an individual investor who watches the value of a nest egg suddenly shrink by 30% or more.

If the Efficient Market Hypothesis is correct in its assumption that securities prices reflect the sum total of all information known by everyone, then this is only true until someone, somewhere changes their mind. The supposition that investment risk can be managed through the independent decisions of each individual investor is premised on the theory that changes in financial market prices are not influenced by the actions of other market participants (think: security specific liquidity risk).

In reality, just the opposite is true. The decisions made by individual investors are greatly affected by the decisions and actions of other investors (think: herding and representativeness). Prices can be driven as much by the dynamics of a crowd as by the rational investment objectives of each individual investor. All types of investment assets can inexplicably become correlated even though each individual investor is receiving information and making investment decisions independently. These decisions and actions can cease to be uncorrelated and instead will occasionally begin to synchronize just like *footsteps on a bridge*. The resulting financial market turbulence produces jaw-dropping, unexpected losses from the unintentional information feedback loop that is driven by our heuristic biases.

Under the right circumstances unexpected news and events have the ability to destabilize markets, but knowing that these circumstances are actually present can only occur after the fact. These fat tail events have a low probability of occurring, but they have large negative consequences.

The probability of thousands of people taking random footsteps and somehow ending up walking in harmony is not zero. Given the right conditions, it is a near certainty. Similarly, unprecedented price moves in financial markets are not once in a lifetime events that are just a result of bad luck. Given the heuristic biases of investors, the probability of a twenty-two standard deviation decline occurring again in financial markets is also not zero.[104]

Financial advisors reinforce the fallacy of market tranquility by framing your risk tolerance as being measured by the choice of either a certain gain or probable gain. A discussion regarding the possibility of large losses is avoided because it may frighten away a potential sale. However, to truly evaluate financial market uncertainty, you must consider both the magnitude and the likelihood of all possible outcomes. This includes not just the good ones, but also the very bad ones. As financial market conditions change for the worse, the willingness of individual investors to bear risk seems to disappear as their *perception* of risk increases and becomes the primary driving force behind the synchronization of investor actions in markets. Trying to reduce your exposure to uncertainty in the midst of financial market turbulence is similar to trying to buy insurance once your house catches on fire.

Ignorance is not bliss in financial markets. An accurate understanding of uncertainty and genuine risks must take into account how you actually make investment decisions, how you will react to changes in financial market volatility and the financial consequences that will result.

Tolerance vs. Perception

Our judgment regarding uncertain outcomes is often wrong. The media, cultural issues and our own past experiences all influence our risk perception. We tend to fear a growing number of relatively minor risks and ignore true threats. Our automatic brain often trumps our logical brain as emotions influence how risk information is processed. Therefore, risk evaluation is not just a function of a projected outcome in objective terms, but also the psychological value of that outcome to the decision maker (think: loss aversion).[105]

Many environments that require risk-taking decisions do not allow you a direct way to link risk to consequence; therefore; you act only on your judgement of a perceived rather than an actual risk. As a result, you often accept different amounts of risk in different contexts or circumstances (think: risk seeking vs. risk avoidance). There is inconsistency in the different levels of risk you perceive among alternate scenarios and you tend to be overly optimistic regarding the outcomes of risks you have not experienced, until a negative result becomes part of your memory.[106]

Investment uncertainty is present anytime there is not a guaranteed investment outcome. Uncertainty can only be transformed to risk when the range, likelihood and value of each possible outcome are known before a choice is made. All these conditions are rarely present in an investment decision making environment.

Establishing your risk tolerance is a focus of the financial advice industry because it is a legal requirement. Risk tolerance is a personality trait and will differ among individual investors. It can be thought of as the amount of uncertainty that an individual investor is willing to accept in the pursuit of an investment goal. Risk perception is the subjective mental evaluation that you make about the severity of a risk. The terms are related, but they are not interchangeable.[107]

Unlike a physical characteristic (think: height) there is no unit of measurement for risk tolerance. Studies confirm that people generally do not accurately estimate their own risk tolerance and their financial advisers' estimates are less accurate than their own.[108]

The standard risk assessment tool used by the financial advice industry is a Know Your Client Form (KYC). Typically, an individual investor will complete the form quickly, often with the assistance of the financial advisor. The general content of the form are questions regarding:

- Your previous types of investments, a basic net worth calculation and an estimate of your annual income.

- Your investment objectives that are a choice between income and capital gains.

- Your investment knowledge as estimated by your financial advisor.

- A general risk tolerance classification as either: low, medium or high.

The KYC may also include an investment strategy category (conservative, balanced or aggressive) that is also determined by your advisor.

Under the KYC risk assessment process, the concept of risk is purposely framed around an imprecise vocabulary. There is not a complete definition of what risk means or the consequences that may result from a classification between the various risk tolerance categories. The perception of risk that is presented to you is always framed in a positive manner (think: income or gains). The word *loss* does not appear. Therefore, your tolerance for risk is established inside a framework that only includes a combination of positive outcomes and your own previous investment experience.

Once you acknowledge the KYC form, the advisor has completed his legal requirements to establish the amount of risk that can be present in your investments. This standard financial advice industry assessment of risk tolerance is highly subjective, and can be strongly influenced by the biases and goals of the advisor completing the form.

Perception and Tolerance

Research (Roszkowski et al 2009) indicates that the risk tolerance of individual investors has long-term stability; however, the perceptions about the riskiness of investments will change with the volatility of financial market conditions.[109]

DALBAR's Quantitative Analysis of Investor Behavior (QAIB) has been measuring the return consequences of investor decisions to purchase and sell U.S. mutual funds since 1984. For the 20 years ending December 31st, 2009, the QAIB showed that the average equity fund investor realized annual returns of 3.17% compared to 8.21% for the S&P 500 Index. These results have shown that the average investor earns significantly less than the returns suggested by the performance histories of mutual funds.

These studies show that investment returns are very dependent on the behaviour of individual investors, as most do not have the patience or emotional wherewithal to tolerate financial market volatility. Equity fund investors typically sell their holdings in less than four years, regardless of their stated investment objectives and time horizons.[110]

The initial experience of a large investment loss is a powerful psychological event for an individual investor. The lack of previous experience has not created a historical evaluation reference point and any discussion of these types of declines are absent from the KYC risk tolerance assessment. A change in the individual investor's risk perception frequently occurs, as the automatic brain is convinced that the future will now mirror the immediate past (think: representativeness). The result is *a sell low and buy high* investment strategy that is fuelled by the changes in the individual investor's perception of risk.

The definition of risk used by the financial advice industry needs to be redefined and made clearer, so that risk tolerance and risk perception become much more closely linked. If risk tolerance is determined correctly when an investment program is established, then financial market volatility should not result in a change in risk perception. What is currently absent is a direct link to the size of investment losses and the ability of the individual investor to withstand these losses.

Risk must be understood in terms of the potential magnitude of declines and the increased likelihood of experiencing within-horizon losses as time horizon increases (think: the path you take will actually determine if you arrive). Individual investors care about losses at every point in their investment time horizon.

Changes in risk perception are a direct result of within-horizon losses reaching critical thresholds. Individual investors frequently change their asset allocation once their portfolios have experienced these unexpected large losses (think: loss aversion and regret). Investment decisions that are made by your automatic brain have crippling effects on investment performance.

The starting point of linking risk to the size of losses is a simple question:

"How much money are you willing to lose in any year?"

This question addresses within-horizon losses directly and also provides a critical loss threshold that can be used as the basis for the asset allocation of your investment portfolio.

Drawdowns

The uncertainty of within-horizon losses is generally ignored by the financial advice industry, as evidenced by the investment strategies it promotes (think: leveraged investing and dollar cost averaging). This is unacceptable, since historical information regarding within-horizon losses is widely available for mutual funds and financial market indexes.

Do you remember the previous discussion on drawdowns?

Drawdown analysis measures the peak-to-trough decline of an investment portfolio. The peak is achieved when the portfolio reaches a new high value, and the drawdown is the period in which the portfolio value is less than the peak. The drawdown is measured from the time a retrenchment begins to the time a new high is reached.

Therefore, a drawdown quantifies two equally important factors for individual investors:

- The size of historical within-horizon losses.

- The length of time required to recover the loss.

Financial market declines can occur at any time and have no fixed length. Individual investors experience declines as they happen, not according to a fixed schedule. Therefore, proper drawdown analysis should be completed using monthly data rather than by using an arbitrary date such as calendar year end.

The following sample portfolios are representative of typical asset mixes that are frequently recommended to individual investors. The investments are diversified internationally and by asset class. The allocation to equities ranges from 30% in Portfolio 1 to 100% in Portfolio 3.

	Cash	Bonds	International Bonds	Canadian Equities	U.S. Equities	International Equities
Portfolio 1	15%	35%	20%	15%	10%	5%
Portfolio 2	10%	15%	5%	30%	20%	20%
Portfolio 3	0%	0%	0%	30%	35%	35%

The drawdowns for each portfolio were calculated on a month-by-month basis from January 1st, 1973 to December 31st, 2010. The tables show the ten largest drawdowns, sorted from the largest percentage decline to the smallest.

Portfolio 1

Size of Decline	Began Declining	Completed Recovery	Months In Decline	Months To Recover
-13.1%	Nov 1973	Jan 1975	11	4
-8.3%	Apr 1981	Oct 1981	6	1
-7.5%	Sep 1987	Sep 1988	3	10
-6.5%	Jan 1990	Oct 1990	4	6
-6.1%	Sep 2000	Apr 2003	10	22
-5.7%	Feb 1994	Jan 1995	5	7
-5.2%	Jan 2009	July 2009	2	5
-5.0%	Feb 1980	Mar 1980	2	1
-4.3%	Sep 2008	Nov 2008	1	2
-4.3%	Oct 1979	Dec 1979	1	2

Source: Index Wealth Management Inc.

Portfolio 2

Size of Decline	Began Declining	Completed Recovery	Months In Decline	Months To Recover
-28.2%	Sep 2000	Nov 2005	31	32
-27.3%	Nov 1973	Dec 1975	11	15
-25.4%	Jun 2007	Nov 2010	21	21
-18.4%	Sep 1987	Mar 1989	3	16
-12.0%	Jan 1990	Jan 1991	9	4
-11.3%	Dec 1980	Sep 1982	20	2
-10.7%	July 1998	Oct 1998	2	2
-8.8%	Mar 1980	May 1980	1	2
-5.9%	Oct 1979	Nov 1979	1	1
-5.4%	Feb 1973	Aug 1973	4	3

Source: Index Wealth Management Inc.

Portfolio 3

Size of Decline	Began Declining	Completed Recovery	Months In Decline	Months To Recover
-42.5%	Sep 2000	Dec 2006	31	45
-40.6%	Jun 2007	*	21	*
-38.2%	Nov 1973	Nov 1976	11	26
-25.3%	Sep 1987	Jun 1989	3	19
-19.9%	Dec 1980	Oct 1982	20	3
-17.8%	Jan 1990	Apr 1991	9	7
-13.1%	July 1998	Oct 1998	2	2
-10.4%	Mar 1980	May 1980	1	2
-7.4%	Feb 1973	Sep 1973	4	4
-6.6%	Oct 1979	Nov 1979	1	1

*recovery is still not complete
Source: Index Wealth Management Inc.

Portfolio performance was calculated by using asset-class total-return indexes as proxies for sector performance. No allowance was made for fees and taxes. Portfolios were rebalanced annually.

The drawdown results for each portfolio allocation provide important information for individual investors:

- Reviewing the frequency, size and recovery times of historical losses ties the concepts of risk tolerance and risk perception together.

- Reviewing the size of the historical declines provides a guideline to access if historical losses exceed what an individual investor would consider to be a critical loss threshold.

- The size of losses and recovery times varies greatly. Large and small losses can both require long periods to recover. These recovery times matter because they reduce the limited period of time available to accumulate capital and experience positive compounding (think: mathematics of losses).

Drawdowns and Capacity

Drawdown analysis combines the important concepts of risk tolerance and risk perspective. However, while it is important to have the emotional ability to tolerate the historical size and frequency of investment losses by not selling your investments during market declines, this does not mean that you also have the financial capacity to recover from these losses even if you continue to hold your investments (think: mathematics of losses; and experience vs. exposure).

Remember that you have two distinct time horizons that occur over their investment life:

- An accumulation phase: where the focus is on saving.

- A withdrawal phase: where the focus is on spending.

In the example of John, he lost 30% of the market value of his portfolio and only had three years left until the start of his retirement. He required a gain of 42.9% to allow his portfolio value to recover to its previous peak valuation.

John's financial advisor concluded that he needs to increase the risk of the investments included in his portfolio in order to produce a projected increased rate of return. Although this strategy may have been consistent with his risk tolerance, she did not consider the negative consequences of a further decline in the value of his investments. There is always a relationship between risk tolerance and risk capacity.

An evaluation of his risk capacity should have shown that even a small further decline in his portfolio value would put his retirement saving goal in further jeopardy (think: mathematics of losses). Risk capacity is an absolute measure that should be used as a reality check of risk tolerance.

John authorized the advisor's investment recommendation based upon the allure of higher returns, and he is ultimately the one who has to live with the outcome. However, the financial advice industry should be held to a better standard of risk disclosure so that individual investors have true informed consent regarding the consequences of the asset allocation that is being recommended for their investments.

Exploring historical portfolio drawdowns is a powerful educational experience that aligns the intangible concepts of risk tolerance, risk perception and risk capacity to allow misconceptions about financial market uncertainty and returns to be corrected.

Investment Success = Abridged Uncertainty - Consequence

I am of the belief that it is not within the capabilities of any individual investor or mutual fund manager to identify equity investments that will have a risk-adjusted, after-cost return that is consistently greater than that of a financial market index (think: heuristic biases, Mandelbrot rules, scaling and power laws). Even if I am wrong and there are a few exceptional fund managers out there somewhere in the investment universe, I don't believe that any individual investor or financial advisor can distinguish in advance these managers from the ones who are simply lucky (think: Bill Miller). In addition, the inherent sales bias that is present in the financial advice industry does not provide any incentive for advisors to admit defeat for active management strategies and to recommend less costly investment alternatives.

To this point, I have only provided the background to support my beliefs, but I have not offered any solutions to readers regarding how to overcome these obstacles to financial success. Uncertainty in financial markets is inevitable. You cannot eliminate all uncertainty; however there are effective ways to achieve degrees of safety. Reducing uncertainty and its consequences will always involve trade-offs. When the elements of this trade-off have been separated, they can be clearly understood and compared.

If You Are So Rich, Why Aren't You Smart?

The financial advice industry doesn't have to be smart to get rich, since they make their money from the fees they convince you to pay. The performance of your investments does very little to affect their compensation. However, reducing investment fees is within your control and will have a direct positive effect on your investment return (think: why investment costs matter and your MER pain threshold).

There is an overwhelming amount of research that shows that the average individual or investment manager who uses an active approach to portfolio management, will fail to outperform a benchmark index (think: the myth of active management).[111]

If you were offered the opportunity to make an investment decision where you knew beforehand that the odds of the projected outcome were stacked heavily in your favour, would you select it?

Individual investors can gain these odds by investing directly in a security that replicates the performance of a financial market index, rather than by selecting an actively managed mutual fund.

Index vs. Active

An index is a statistical compilation of the prices of a number of representative securities. Indexes are defined by the types of investments they include, such as equities, bonds or commodities.

A *composite index* is the one that includes all securities listed on an exchange (think: S&P/TSX Composite Index). The purpose of a composite index is to act as a proxy for the performance of all the securities listed on the exchange.

The formula to determine the value of most composite indexes is usually based on the weighted capitalization of the securities included in the index. Therefore, companies with larger market values make up a larger portion of the index value than smaller capitalization companies. As a result, the future price changes of each security will affect their proportional representation (think: winners get larger, losers get smaller). The securities included will only change because of mergers, acquisitions or changes in circumstances that make them no longer eligible for inclusion.[112]

Index investing is designed to replicate as closely as possible the investment return that is produced by an underlying index. This is achieved by holding an investment that contains all the securities, in the same proportions, as those that are included in the index.

Canada's first index investment was National Trust's TSE 300 Index Fund that was created in 1978.[113]

As investor awareness of the benefits of index investing increased, Exchange Traded Funds (ETFs) began to be introduced in 1990. Unlike index funds, which require purchases and redemptions to be made through a fund manufacturer, ETFs are units of a trust that are listed and trade on financial exchanges. Canadian assets in ETFs have increased from approximately $5 billion in 2002 to close to $32.5 billion by the end of 2009. ETFs are now available that track almost all indexes that are used in Canada and around the globe.[114]

ETFs now provide a better investment alternative to index funds, since index funds will generally have greater internal costs. The open ended structure of index funds requires them to incur costs for administration and unit holder transactions. Index funds also must endure trading and market impact costs for portfolio rebalancing that is required because of requested unit holder transactions.

Beware Wolves in Sheep's Clothing

The financial advice industry cannot stay rich by advising individual investors to buy index funds and rebalance their portfolios every six months. However, they know a good thing when they see it and so there is a growing attempt to capitalize on the popularity of ETFs by marketing *Actively Managed ETFs*.

Manufactures are now creating ETFs with objectives that require holding only some securities that are included in an index or that track the active security selections of a portfolio manager. There are also ETFs with embedded leverage that attempt to provide two or three times the daily return of a benchmark index. These strategies are designed to *improve* on the idea of index investing. However, they also require increased management fees and trading, which reduces many of the advantages of tax efficiency and minimal tracking error that are gained from a traditional ETF security.

What individual investors are actually being sold is the concept of active management disguised as an ETF, which eliminates the odds of the projected outcome that you had in your favour (think: the myth of active management). Why would you be willing to make this bet?

The Quest for Safety

"Rather than asking what can go right, ask what can go wrong"

Benjamin Graham

The precautionary principle is an approach to risk management that has been developed for dealing with circumstances of scientific uncertainty. This reflects the need to take prudent action in the face of a potentially serious risk. This principal is becoming increasingly prominent in environmental and health issues that require the management of risks that evolve over time.

The main theme of the precautionary principal is to encourage the prevention or mitigation of an evolving risk. Therefore, decision making must take into account the important characteristics of a problem: a long time horizon, shifting uncertainties, the potential for unexpected shocks and the irreversibility of negative consequences. It requires the need by a decision maker to anticipate and quantify harm before it occurs.

Financial market prices are random and unpredictable (think: Mandelbrot rules, scaling and power laws). The financial advice industry equates price volatility to risk. This is nonsense. Risk isn't volatility, it is price volatility that leads to a permanent loss of your investment capital (think: risk = uncertainty x consequence). Frequently to individual investors, the negative consequences of financial market uncertainty are irreversible (think: risk capacity and mathematics of losses). However, if unpredictable price volatility is hedged against in advance, then the permanent loss of your investment capital can be avoided. Therefore, the need to indemnify financial market uncertainty should be a central theme in your investment process.

Insurance is often a neglected asset in investing, because the financial advice industry generally sells investment insurance only as part of structured investment products. The four most common types are:

- **A Segregated Fund**, which is a mutual fund that will guarantee a minimum of 75% to 100% of the initial investment value if it is held to a maturity date (usually ten years). A segregated fund will also pay a guaranteed minimum value in the event that the individual investor dies. The cost of this guarantee is expensive as most segregated funds charge an additional MER of 3% in *addition* to the regular MER of the underlying fund (think: total MERs over 5%).

- **A Life Annuity Contract** requires the payment of capital to an insurance company in exchange for the guarantee that the insurance company will make periodic payments to the annuitant for life. These payments can have a guaranteed minimum time period, such as ten years. However, after the expiry of this period the payments cease upon the death of the annuitant, regardless of the total amount of payments that the annuitant received.

- **A Guaranteed Minimum Withdrawal Benefit Annuity** (GMWB) allows the annuitant to withdraw a maximum percentage of their investment value each year. In general, GMWBs allow your portfolio to be invested in mutual funds to a maximum allocation of 70% equities. The cost of this guarantee can be expensive (think: total MERs over 4%).

- **Principal Protected Notes and Market-Linked GICs** allow an individual investor to receive a return that is based on the performance of a financial market index, commodity or mutual fund. They guarantee a minimum return of principal if held to the typical maturity of three to seven years (think: loss aversion appeal). However, they also have an embedded sales commission of 5%; annual MER expenses of over 3%; a return formula that is often capped compared to the underlying security that performance is based upon; and are not covered for default protection of the issuer.

The financial advice industry has mastered the art of transforming simple concepts into overly complex investment products. As a result, the costs associated with these types of products make the insurance benefit largely unappealing.

Margins of investment safety can be achieved by hedging uncertainty with much less expensive types of insurance. These strategies can protect your capital and will allow you to respond to unexpected financial market outcomes. This requires the development of a sequential investment approach, so that throughout your investment horizon you have ownership of an *option* that will allow you the opportunity to revise your investment decisions as your progress toward achieving your financial goals.

First, Do No Harm

Do you remember John? He had three years to go before starting retirement and he had just lost 30% of the value of his portfolio. He was worried. He knew that his investments were between a rock and a hard place. His accumulation phase was nearing an end and his spending phase was about to begin. He now realized that he had to receive a return of 42.9% just to get back to where he began two years ago. He could not experience any further significant declines in the value of his portfolio and still expect to receive the investment income he required to support his retirement lifestyle.

This stark reality gave him the motivation to spend more time educating himself about financial market uncertainty and the financial advice industry.

His previous investment experiences proved to him that financial markets were much more uncertain than what he had previously believed, or what his advisors had explained to him. His advisors always made their investment recommendations based on either historical mutual fund performance or their future projected rates of return of these funds. He now realized that basing investment decisions on either of these factors did not lead to above average investment returns. In fact, the opposite was true. Chasing performance meant that he frequently sold and bought investments at the wrong times.

He also now understood how his financial advisors were paid from fees and commissions that were hidden inside these funds. Why weren't these fees more clearly shown to him before he accepted their advice? He did not begrudge anyone earning a living, but he would have asked more questions about why the funds were recommended had he known how much of his money was being paid as commissions and trailer fees to his advisors.

He had read more about ETFs and index investing and their superior long-term performance compared to most actively managed mutual funds. He now appreciated how reducing the fees he paid would add directly to the returns he received in his portfolio. If his advisors were truly focused on providing him with the best financial advice, why didn't they show him ETF investments as a comparison to actively managed mutual funds and let him make an informed choice?

When market losses suddenly appeared, or the performance of his investments was less than the advisors projected, they seemed to be just as surprised by the results as him. His advisors always told him to *be patient and prices would come back*. The risk tolerance assigned to him by his advisors always seemed to be based on the amount of patience they believed he had to wait for these recoveries after the downturns. They never mentioned that these waiting periods could take years and would erode the limited time he had to accumulate capital through positive compounding of his investments. He had accepted every recommendation they made and waited patiently, but he had not reached his investment goal and was close to running out of time.

He understood that to receive returns he needed to assume risk, but he always seemed to receive more "risk" than "return". Who knew that a series of losses on derivatives by a small Spanish bank that he had never heard of could cause a 30% drop in his portfolio value in one week? If financial markets were that fragile, why was there not some way available to truly protect the value of his investments from these unexpected events?

John had recently paid the annual premium for his home insurance. Every year he renewed this insurance to protect the value of his home against an unexpected event that could cause serious harm to its value. Why couldn't he buy insurance for his investment portfolio like he did for his house? His portfolio seemed to suffer more frequent calamities than his house. He would be more than willing to pay a premium like he does for house insurance and protect his portfolio from future harm.

Better Safe, Than Sorry

Experience is based on previous history and considers the probability of future outcomes only in the context of what has previously occurred. *Exposure* considers *both* the past history and the potential for any future outcome that has never previously occurred.

Drawdown analysis is a useful exercise for individual investors to illustrate histori-cal performance of a portfolio asset allocation. However, it assumes that past experi-ence will also be the worst performance that can be expected in the future. This ignores the fact that market crashes always seem to set a new precedent for declines.

Exposure management eliminates, or substantially reduces, the consequences that are the result of financial market uncertainty. When properly structured, it has a similar function to that of asset allocation. You decide on a desired risk/return level for your investments, and exposure management ensures that your investment performance tracks these objectives, while reducing or eliminating exposure to unanticipated shocks. Investment asset allocation is typically *static* (think: constant over long time horizons), whereas exposure management is an inherently dynamic activity.

Exposure management has a short-term term focus within a long-term invest-ment horizon. It is accomplished by trading either cash payments or potential future return for pre-established degrees of safety that offset future financial market uncer-tainty (think: insurance). This leads to an ongoing process of short-term protection and revision as you proceed toward achieving your long-term investment goals. If you *hedge* against uncertainty in advance, then the consequences of a permanent loss of your investment capital can be avoided.

Consider Your Options

Listed options are securities that can be used to reduce financial market uncertainty.

An option is a contract with defined terms that gives the buyer the right, but not the obligation, to buy or sell an investment at a specific price on or before a certain date.

There are two types of options:

- Calls: which give the holder the right to buy an asset at a certain price within a specific period of time.

- Puts: which give the holder the right to sell an asset at a certain price within a specific period of time.

In return for granting the option, called *writing*, the originator of the option col-lects a payment, called the *premium*, from the buyer. The writer of an option must make good on delivering (or receiving) the underlying asset if the option is exercised. Options are traded on financial exchanges and have a central clearing facility that guarantees the terms of the contract. Contract terms range from one month to two years and are available for many ETFs and most individual listed equity securities. Options are not available for actively managed mutual funds.

Put options are a form of insurance, which guarantees the price at which an investment may be sold during a period of time. Like other forms of insurance, a put will reduce your exposure to adverse financial outcomes, in exchange for the payment of a premium.

Purchasing put options can provide a spectrum of protection against losses in the market value of your portfolio. By purchasing a put option you can link your risk tolerance and risk perspective directly to your risk capacity through an insurance contract. For example, you may decide that losses greater than 10% are unacceptable over any six month time period. Accepting the first 10% of a loss is analogous to the *deductible* that is part of your home insurance policy. Losses beyond 10% can be protected against by purchasing a put option that will become effective 10% below the current market value of your portfolio.

ETFs + Options = > Uncertainty

John has decided to use his new knowledge about financial market uncertainty and the financial advice industry to his advantage. He will sell his mutual fund investments to eliminate the MER charges he is paying and will reinvest the proceeds in an ETF.

He chose an ETF that replicates the performance of a broad market composite index. By reviewing the investment holdings of his mutual funds, he discovered that many of the equities were also included in the same index. However, the fund charged an MER of 2.53% compared to 0.17% for the ETF. This cost savings would add directly to his investment performance.

John realized that, with only three years to retirement, his previous 30% portfolio loss had greatly reduced his risk capacity. To protect against another catastrophic loss in his portfolio he purchased a six month put option based upon the value of his ETF investment. This option becomes effective if the market price of the ETF has declined by more than 10% over the next six months. The premium John paid to purchase this insurance was 2.5% of the initial market value of the ETF, but he will receive all the dividends and any capital appreciation from the ETF over this time period.

At the end of six months, the put option contract will expire and there are three possible outcomes:

- **The ETF Appreciates** – At expiration, if the price of the ETF increases then the put will have no value. The return John receives from the appreciation of the ETF and the dividends will offset the cost of the put premium. However, in exchange for the cost of the put, John knew with certainty the maximum loss that he could experience in his investment portfolio.

- **The ETF Declines By More Than 10%** – At expiration, if the price of the ETF has declined by more than 10%, the price of the put will be equal to the value of the loss that exceeds 10%. For example, if the price of the ETF has declined by 20%, then the put value would offset 10% of this decline. In exchange for the cost of the put, John has limited the maximum loss in his portfolio to his maximum risk capacity.

- **The ETF Declines By Less Than 10%** – At expiration, if the price of the ETF has declined by less than 10%, the put will have no value. For example, if the price of the ETF declined by 5%, the put will expire worthless. In exchange for the cost of the put, John limited the maximum loss in his portfolio to his maximum risk capacity, but did not receive any compensation for the small loss experienced by his portfolio.

ETFs + Options = + Cash

Writing a covered *call* option allows an individual investor to trade the *potential* future appreciation of an investment (that may or may not occur) in exchange for cash today.

By selling a call option, the writer agrees to sell the underlying investment that the option is based upon, at a certain price and within a specific period of time. The call option writer is paid a cash premium for granting the purchaser the right to buy the underlying investment.

The trade-off for writing the call option and receiving the premium is that the writer agrees to limit the potential appreciation that is retained from the underlying investment over the time period covered by the option contract.

A year has passed since John made his ETF investment and began using put options to protect the value of his portfolio. The first put option he purchased proved valuable, as the market had a sharp decline almost immediately after he made his initial ETF investment. He found it much easier to *be patient and wait for the price to recover* knowing that he had protected against further declines if the financial markets continued to weaken. The price of the ETF eventually rebounded strongly and, as a result, the second put option that he purchased expired worthless as the insurance was not needed.

John has become more comfortable with option securities and their ability to hedge against financial market uncertainty. He then wanted to use the volatility of financial markets to his advantage in his option strategies. He still wanted to own puts to protect against losses, but he discovered that he could trade the cash premiums he received in exchange for limiting the future appreciation of his ETF to pay for the cost of his put protection.

To protect against another catastrophic loss in his portfolio, he purchased another six month put option based upon the current value of his ETF. This option becomes effective if the market price of his ETF declines by more than 10% over the next six months. To pay the premium for the put insurance, John also sells a call option that limits the price appreciation of the ETF to 6% over the same time period. The premium he receives from selling the call now offsets the premium he must pay for buying the put, so he no longer needs to have cash available to protect his ETF investment. He will also continue to receive all the dividends paid by the ETF over the contract period.

At the end of six months, the put and call option contracts will expire and there are three possible outcomes:

- **The ETF Appreciates By More Than 6%** — At expiration, if the price of the ETF increases by more than 6% then the put will have no value and expire. The return John receives from the appreciation of the ETF will be limited to 6% by the call option, and he will still retain the dividends paid. Since the cost of the put was paid by selling the call, John knew with certainty the maximum loss that he could experience in his investment portfolio and also the maximum potential return.

- **The ETF Declines By More Than 10%** – At expiration, if the price of the ETF has declined by more than 10%, the price of the put will be equal to the value of the loss that exceeds 10%. The call option will expire worthless. Since the cost of the put was paid from selling the call, John received this protection without any direct cash outlay and still retained the dividends paid by the ETF.

- **The ETF Appreciates By Less Than 6% And Does Not Decline By More Than 10%** – At expiration, if the price of the ETF has declined by less than 10% and also did not appreciate by more than 6%, then both the put and call contracts will expire worthless. John will receive whatever the actual ETF return was within this -10% to 6% range. In this scenario, John did not experience any opportunity cost by entering into the option contracts. The return he received would be identical to that of holding the unhedged ETF, yet he still had protection against a catastrophic loss throughout the period.

A Bird in Your Hand

Another two years passed and John's retirement date arrived. What he was dreading three years ago had now become a time of excitement. His portfolio recovered from the 30% loss and the option strategies he used during the recovery allowed him to worry less about financial market uncertainty and instead plan how he was going to travel during his retirement. He wanted to expand upon his enjoyment for golf by spending several months each year in warmer climates so that he could play more.

However, he would need a stable source of income over the next few years to pay for this travel. His only sources of guaranteed retirement income were the government sponsored Canada Pension Plan and Old Age Security. He had transferred his private pension plan assets into his RRSP almost a decade ago, so his he would have to rely on his investments to produce the bulk of his retirement income.

Even with the call and put strategies he was using, John knew that the returns he was receiving did vary from year to year. Switching a portion of his equity ETF investment to bonds and GICs would reduce the volatility of his investment returns, but the low interest rates these types of investments currently produced seemed like a steep price to pay for a more stable return.

John's tolerance for risk had always been stable throughout his pre-retirement saving period; however his capacity to accept risk declined when his portfolio suffered the 30% loss. Now that this capital had been recovered, he once again had the financial capacity to tolerate greater amounts of portfolio volatility. What he required was a way to use options strategies to provide a stable source of income and some partial protection against future market declines.

John had been purchasing put options to protect against another catastrophic loss in his portfolio and had been writing call options to pay for this protection. If he stopped purchasing the puts and continued writing the calls, he could retain the entire call premium in his account. This meant that he would have additional cash that could be used for either spending during his retirement or to partially offset any declines that may occur in the market value of his ETF investment.

John began writing six month call options that gave the purchaser the right to receive all the potential appreciation of the ETF over a six month time period. The premium he received from selling the call was now 7% and he continued to receive all the dividends paid by the ETF over the contract period. John decided to delay his first trip for six months so he could evaluate the results of his new strategy.

At the end of six months, the call option contract would expire with two possible outcomes:

- **The ETF Appreciates** – John obtained a 7% cash premium when the contract was initiated and any dividends paid over the term. This is the maximum return that he can receive. At expiration, if the price of the ETF increases by more than 7% then John will have forgone any appreciation above this level. However, if the ETF price appreciated by less than 7%, then his return would be greater than that of holding an unhedged ETF over the same period of time.

- **The ETF Depreciates** – At expiration, if the price of the ETF has declined then John will have the value of the cash premium and any dividends received to offset the loss. Therefore, the first 7% the ETF price decline will not result in a loss of capital in his portfolio. However, John will not have any protection for a loss greater than 7%.

Over the next six months there was very little volatility in financial markets. When the call option contract expired, the ETF price was 1% lower than when the contract was initiated and the ETF also paid a 1% dividend over this period. An individual investor who held this ETF investment without any option hedging would have received a zero return. However, John received a 7% return since the call premium and the dividend received offset the 1% depreciation in the price of the ETF.

After some initial budgeting, John realized that he would not need the full amount of the call premiums he was receiving to cover travel expenses. Therefore, he could still use some of the premiums to purchase puts. This protection would not cover the entire value of his ETF investment, but it would provide some partial insurance for his portfolio against any future twenty-two standard deviation market declines that might occur. John's investment experience in financial markets had taught him that he would certainly live through one of these events again someday, because he now understood that anything can occur in financial markets and eventually will!

Success = Exposure Management (Abridged Uncertainty – Consequence)

"Even the most brilliant mathematical geniuses will never be able to tell us what the future holds. In the end, what matters is the quality of our decisions in the face of uncertainty."

Peter L Bernstein, economist and money manager

Even though most individual investors have a basic comprehension of what they should do for their own financial well-being, most will:

- Repeatedly make their own poor investment decisions (think: heuristic biases);

- Or abdicate the responsibility for making their investment decisions to the financial advice industry without a true understanding of the consequences of that decision (think: misinformation and misunderstanding).

Individual investors do not make a conscious choice to fail to achieve their investment goals. However, the evidence from both financial market history and behavioural finance is not encouraging when it comes to supporting the idea that we learn from our mistakes.

Making better investment decisions that will increase your odds of investment success can occur through the knowledge and practice of the following key concepts:

- The prices of securities in financial markets are random. Consequently, they are much more volatile and uncertain than you and most financial advisors perceive.

- These prices are driven by the combined actions of all market participants and they can suddenly and seemingly without warning take on a reality all their own.

- Watch for the misinformation and misunderstanding that is used by the financial advice industry:

    - The historical track records of active management and projections of future performance are illusions that are used to convince you to investment your capital.

    - Borrowing money to purchase mutual funds is a strategy that is skewed against you.

    - How information is presented to you can greatly influence your perception of what it conveys.

- Understand that reducing your investment costs and turnover will lead to increased investment performance.

- The mathematics of investment losses matter. If you choose to put your investment capital at *risk*, make sure you understand the actual risk you are accepting. Your tolerance, perception and capacity for risk are intertwined.

Financial markets are environments where your choices are subjective and made without the benefit of knowing precise mathematical odds or certain outcomes. Your primary investment focus should be to understand the implications of financial market uncertainty and then mitigate the consequences of your exposure through an investment process.

As random changes in financial market conditions unfold, being hedged against declines that are beyond your risk capacity will protect you from the permanent loss of your investment capital. The effective use of option-enhanced investment strategies can provide you with investment certainty and protect you from the heuristic biases that affect your investment decisions.

There are discretionary portfolio management firms and qualified advisors who have the expertise and skill to assist you to implement effective risk adjusted investment strategies. Make sure that you:

- Receive your advice from a fiduciary, not a salesperson.

- Understand the motivations, conflicts and the duty that your financial advisor owes to you.

- Obtain a disclosure regarding the cost of advice, in advance of acting on any investment recommendation.

Asking what can go right with your investments is the wrong question. Ask what can go wrong, and then hedge against it. If you have conviction about your investment decisions and protection from negative consequences, then you can be confident in reaching your investment goals.

INDEX

NOTES

Chapter 1 - Neurons, Electrochemicals And Water

[1]   Samuil Blinkov and Il'ya Glezer (1968) *The Human Brain In Figures and Tables. A Quantitative Handbook new york Press*

[2]   (http://en.wikipedia.org/wiki/Cognition)

[3]   *Joshua Green & Jonathan Cohen. Princeton University. http://www.wired.com/medtech/health/news)*

[4]   *Jason Zweig (2007)Your Money &Your Brain,* Simon & Shuster

[5]   *Antonio Damasio (1995) Descartes Error Quill Harper Collins Publishing pgs 212-222*

[6]   *Antonio Damasio (1995) Descartes Error Quill Harper Collins Publishing pgs 212-222*

Chapter 2 - Your Investing Brain

[7]   *http://www.newworldencyclopedia.org/entry/Muller-Lyer_illusion*

[8]   *R.P Bagozzi, U.M. Dholakia, S. Basuroy (2003) How Effortful Decisions Get Enhanced Journal Of Behavioral Decision Making 16 pgs 273-295*

[9]   *Daniel Tversky Amos Kahneman (1973) Availability: A heuristic for judging frequency and probability Cognitive Psychology*

[10]   *http://en.wikipedia.org/wiki/CNBC*

[11] *Daniel Tversky and Amos Kahneman (1973) Availability: A heuristic for judging frequency and probability. Cognitive Psychology*

[12] *P. Slovic, et al (2002) The Affect Heuristic, Heuristic and Biases: The Psychology of Intuitive Judgment*

[13] *David Hirshleifer and Tyler Shumway (2001) Good Day Sunshine: Stock Returns and Weather Dice Center Working paper No. 2001-3*

[14] *B. Fischhoff et al., (1978) How Safe Is Enough? Policy Sciences 9 pgs127-152*

[15] *B. Fischhoff et al., (1978) How Safe Is Enough? Policy Sciences 9 pgs 127-152*

[16] *Brad M. Barber and Terrance Odean (1999) Boys will be boys: gender, overconfidence and common stock investment The Quarterly Journal of Economics February 2001*

[17] *H. K. Baker and J.R. Nofsinger (2002) Psychological biases of investors, Financial Services Review 11 pgs 97-116*

[18] *Robert Shiller (1992) Market Volatility MIT Press pgs 388-390, 399*

[19] *Bank of Canada http://www.bankofcanada.ca/en/rates/inflation_calc.html*

[20] *Alan Greenspan Humphrey Hawkins Report July 22 1997*

[21] *Clifford Asness Fight the Fed Model Journal of Portfolio Management Fall 2003*

[22] *Charles MacKay (1980) Extraordinary Popular Delusions and the Madness of Crowds Three Rivers Press*

[23] *Terrance Odean (1998) Are investors reluctant to realize their losses? Journal of Finance 53, pgs 1775-1798*

[24] *Daniel Tversky and Amos Kahneman (1981) The Framing of Decisions and the Psychology of Choice. Science. Vol 211(4481) pgs.453-458*

[25] *Carlos Garcia de Andoain (2009) Longwood University, ASBBS Annual Conference February*

[26]   Frank H. Knight (1921) *Risk, Uncertainty, and Profit. Boston, MA: Hart, Schaffner and Marx; Houghton Mifflin Company*

[27]   Daniel Ellsberg (1961) *Risk, Ambiguity, and the Savage Axioms.* Quarterly Journal of Economics 75 (4): pgs 643–669

Chapter 3 - Mathematics + Uncertainty ≠ Risk

[28]   Leonard Mlodinow (2008) *The Drunkard's Walk Pantheon books pg 175*

[29]   Leonard Mlodinow (2008) *The Drunkard's Walk Pantheon books pg ix*

[30]   Ellen Langer and Jane Roth (1975) *Heads I win, tails its chance: The Illusion of Control as a Function of the Sequence of Outcomes in a Purely Chance task. Journal of Personality and Social Psychology (32:6), pgs 951-955*

[31]   Jason Zweig (2007) *Your Money &Your Brain Simon & Shuster pg 46*

[32]   D. Biswas G. Zhao D.R. Lehmann (2011) *The Impact of Sequential Data on Consumer Confidence in Relative Judgments. Journal of Consumer Research: February 2011*

[33]   Bureau of Labour Statistics, U.S. Department of Labour

[34]   Hersh Shefrin (2007) *Behavioral Finance: Biases, Mean-variance Returns, and Risk Premiums. CFA Institute Conference Proceedings June 2007*

[35]   Philip Shane, Boochun Jung, SunnyYang, (September 2009) *Do Financial Analysts' Long-term Growth Forecasts Reflect Effective Effort Towards Informative Stock Recommendations? Available at SSRN: http://ssrn.com/abstract=1466413*

[36]   R. Hertwig et al (2003) *Decisions from experience and the effect of rare events in risky choice Psychological Science Volume 15 Number 8 pgs 534-536*

[37]   Grant McQueen Steven Thorley (1999) *Mining Fool's Gold Marriott School of Management BrighamYoung University*

[38]   Grant McQueen Steven Thorley (1999) *Mining Fool's Gold Marriott School of Management BrighamYoung University*

[39]   *Leonard Koppett (1978) Carrying Statistics to Extremes Sporting News*

[40]   *Peter Bernstein (1996) Against The Gods The Remarkable Story of Risk John Wiley & Sons pg 334*

Chapter 4 - Financial Markets Suppositions

[41]   *T. Zaleskiewz (2001) Beyond Risk Seeking & Risk Aversion. European Journal of Personality pgs 105 -122*

[42]   *A.C.D Donkers and V.H.O. Van Soest (1997) Subjective Measures Of Household Preferences and Financial Decisions 1997-70 Tiburg University Centre for Economic Research*

[43]   *https://www.ism-chicago.org/insidepages/reportsonbusiness*

[44]   *http://www.irwebreport.com/daily/2010/08/03/investors-get-news-80-seconds-after-wall-street/*

[45]   *Bank of International Settlements June 2010*

[46]   *ISDA Research Notes Concentration of OTC Derivatives Among Major Dealers Issue 4, 2010*

[47]   *Fred Dopfel (2003) On the implications of lower stock-bond correlations Journal of Portfolio Management, v. 30, issue 1, pp. 25-38*

[48]   *Antti Ilmanen (2003) Stock Bond Correlations The Journal of Fixed Income September 2003, Vol. 13, No. 2: pp. 55-66*

[49]   *Y. Amihud et al (2005) Liquidity and Asset Prices Pedersen Foundations and Trends in Finance, 2005, vol.1, no. 4, pp. 269-364*

[50]   *Stephen Morris et al (2003) Liquidity Black Holes November 21, 2003 London School of Economics*

[51]   *U.S. Conference Board January 22, 2007*

[52]   *Roger Lowenstein (2000) When Genius Failed, Random House*

[53]   *Benoit Mandelbrot (2004) The (Mis)Behaviour of Financial Markets Basic Books pgs 145-149*

54 *http://www.emini-maven.com/wordpress/2008/08/benoit-mandelbrots-pioneering-fractal-and-chaos-theory*

55 *Benoit Mandelbrot (2004) The (Mis) Behavior of Financial Markets Basic Books pgs 20-24, 225-252 2004 15*

56 *Albert-Laszlo Barabasi (1999) Emergence of Scaling in Random Networks University of Notre Dame*

Chapter 5 – The Financial Advice Industry: Costs, Conflicts and Camouflage

57 *Government of Canada Department of Finance June 2005*

58 *Government of Canada Department of Finance Canada's Mutual Fund Industry March 2002*

59 *Fund Library.com Canada's Mutual Fund Database*

60 *Jamie Dunkley (2009) FSA plans ban commission for financial advisors June 2009 The Telegraph*

61 *A. Turner 2010 Chairman FSA Mansion House Speech London September 21 2010*

62 *Risk Insurance Escapes Commission Ban April 27 2010 insurancenews.com.au*

63 *Langdon (2010) Lurching Toward Disclosure Investment Executive Magazine October 18 2010*

64 *Langdon (2010) Lurching Toward Disclosure Investment Executive Magazine October 18 2010*

65 *http://dictionary.reference.com/browse/fiduciary*

66 *http://www.ifse.ca*

67 *Khorana, Servaves, Tufano (2007) Mutual Fund Fees Around the World Oxford University Press for Society for Financial Studies Vol. 22 Issue 3 March 2009 pgs 1279-1310*

68 *Lamb (2010) Canadian fund costs in line with the U.S. Sept 9 2010 www.advisor.ca*

[69]   *Gordon Powers F-Class mutual funds fail to take the market by storm Investment Executive November 13, 2007*

[70]   *G. Kadlec R. Edelen R. Evans (September 2006) Scale Effects in Mutual Fund Performance: The Role of Trading Costs*

[71]   *Choi Laibson Madrian (2009)Why Does the Law of One Price Fail? An Experiment on Index Mutual Funds 2009 Oxford University Press*

[72]   *Harvard Business School (2006) Assessing the Costs and Benefits of Brokers in the Mutual Fund Industry*

[73]   *Jones, Lessieg, Smythe (2005) Financial advisors and multiple share class mutual funds Financial Services Review, 14, pgs 1-20*

[74]   *Daniel Bergstresser, John Chalmers, Peter Tufano Assessing the Costs and Benefits of Brokers in the Mutual Fund Industry Review of Financial Studies 22, no. 10 (October 2009): 4129–4156*

[75]   *M.J. Roszkowski G.E. Snelbecker (1990) Effects of "framing" on measures of risk tolerance: Financial planners are not immune. The Journal of Behavioral Economics, 1990;19:237–246*

[76]   *AUSTRALIAN JOURNAL OF MANAGEMENT Special Issue, March 2008 – 550*

[77]   *Standard & Poors Index vs. Active Scorecard Second Quarter June 30/2010*

[78]   *http://www.morningstar.ca/globalhome/industry/news.asp?articleid=ArticleID421200510301*

[79]   *Cawfield (2002) On track to extend his winning streak to 12 calendar years Morningstar.ca*

[80]   *Riva Atlas (2005) Securing the streak December 30, 2005 New York Times*

[81]   *Leonard Lodinow (2008) the Drunkard's Walk Random House pgs 179-181*

[82]   *Andy Gogerty (2008) Mutual Fund Red Flags Nov 2008 morningstar.com*

[83]   *M.M. Carhart (1997) On Persistence in Mutual Fund Performance The Journal of Finance, Vol. 52, No. 1 (Mar., 1997), pp. 57-82*

[84]   *Russel Kinnel (2004) Studying the New Star Rating November 22, 2004, 42002 Morningstar.com*

[85]   *Guercio and Tkac (2001) Federal Reserve Bank of Atlanta Working Paper 2001-15 August 2001*

[86]   *Jain and Wu (2000) Truth in Mutual Fund Advertising: Evidence on Future Performance and Fund Flows Journal of Finance 2000, vol. 55, issue 2, pages 937-958*

[87]   *Mullainathan and Shleifer (2005) Persuasion in Finance Harvard University October 2005*

[88]   *Guercio and Tkac Federal Reserve Bank of Atlanta Working Paper 2001-15 August 2001*

[89]   *Jain and Wu (2000) Truth in Mutual Fund Advertising: Evidence on Future Performance and Fund Flows Journal of Finance 2000, vol. 55, issue 2, pages 937-958*

[90]   *William Sharp (1991) The Arithmetic of Active Management The Financial Analysts' Journal Vol. 47, No. 1, January/February 1991 pp. 7-9*

[91]   *Carhart et al (August 9 2001) MUTUAL FUND SURVIVORSHIP Quantitative Strategies, Goldman Sachs Asset Management*

[92]   *Standard & Poors SPIVA Scorecard Year End 2009*

[93]   *G.M. Constantinides (1979) A note on the Sub optimality of Dollar-Cost Averaging as an Investment Policy Journal of Financial and Quantitative Analysis, Volume 14, Issue 2 Jun 1979 pgs 443-450*

[94]   *P. Bacon and Fall Ainina (1997) Does Dollar Cost Averaging Work For Bonds Journal of Financial Planning Vol. 10 No. 3 pgs 78-80*

[95]   *Lewis Mandel and John Knight (1993) Nobody Gains from Dollar Cost Averaging Analytical, Numerical and Empirical Results Financial Services Review 2(1): 5 1-61*

[96]   *M. Kritzman and D. Risk (2002) The Mismeasurement of Risk Financial Analysis Journal, May/June 2002*

[97]   *MFDA Member Regulation Notice MR-0006 MR-0074 Leverage Risk Disclosure May 19, 2010*

[98]   *btobtrust.com/borrowtoinvest*

[99]   *M. Kritzman and D. Risk (2002) The Mismeasurement of Risk Financial Analysts Journal, May/June 2002*

[100] *Ian Hacking (1980) Strange Expectations Philosophy of Science 47: 562-567*

[101] *Paul A. Samuelson Risk and Uncertainty: A Fallacy of Large Numbers The Collected Scientific Papers of Paul A. Samuelson, ed. Joseph E. Stiglitz (Cambridge: MIT Press, 1966), 153-8*

Chapter 6 - Your Way Forward: A Better Approach To Financial Market Uncertainty

[102] *Explaining Why The Millennium Bridge Wobbled Science Daily Nov 3 2005*

[103] *Army Study Guide Steps & Marching http://www.armystudyguide.com/content/Prep_For_Basic_Training/prep_for_basic_drill_and_ceremony/steps-and-marching.shtml*

[104] *Danielsson and Shin (September 2002) Endogenous Risk London School of Economics*

[105] *Dan Gardner (2008) Risk: The Science and Politics of Fear McClelland & Stewart pgs 16-8*

[106] *F.P.McKenna and I.P.Albery (2001) Does Unrealistic Optimism Change following a Negative Experience? Journal of Applied Social Psychology 31 : 1146–1157*

[107] *D.R. Hunter (2002) Risk Perception and Risk Tolerance in Aircraft Pilots, Report No.: DOT/FAA/AM-02/17 Washington, DC: Office of Aerospace Medicine, Federal Aviation Administration*

[108] *Risk Tolerance Revisited, FinaMetrica White Paper, April 2009, www.riskprofiling.com/Downloads/GD_RR.pdf*

[109] *M.J. Roszkowski and D.M. Cordell (2009) A Longitudinal Perspective on Financial Risk Tolerance: Rank-Order and Mean Level Stability International Journal of Behavioural Accounting and Finance 1 (2009): 111–134*

[110] *March 2010 QAIB Dalbar Inc. 600 Atlantic Ave Boston MA 02210*

[111] *Standard & Poors Index Versus Active Scorecard Second Quarter June 30/2010*

[112] *Blitzer Index Mathematics Standard & Poors Dec 14 2005*

[113] *Eric Kirzner (2000) Fact and Fantasy in Index Investing Rotman School of Management, University of Toronto*

[114] *The basics of iShares ETFs www.ca.iShares.com*

Made in the USA
Charleston, SC
09 April 2013